*Kreskin's Fun Way
to Mind Expansion*

Kreskin's Fun Way to Mind Expansion

MENTAL TECHNIQUES YOU CAN MASTER

By Kreskin

DOUBLEDAY & COMPANY, INC.
GARDEN CITY, NEW YORK
1984

Library of Congress Cataloging in Publication Data

Kreskin, 1935–
    Kreskin's Fun way to mind expansion.

    1. Conjuring.   2.Thought-transference.   3. Extra-
sensory perception.   I. Title.   II. Title: Fun way to
mind expansion.
GV1553.K74   1984   793.8   82–45358
ISBN 0-385-18246-5

TO BOB COLLINS,
SY FISH, AND RAY PORTER,
WHOSE COMRADESHIP AND COUNSEL
HAVE EASED MY JOURNEYS
OVER TROUBLED WATERS

Contents

Preface

Preparing this, my third book, has been like giving birth to a baby—and like a baby, it has two parents. Robert Bahr is gifted both as a writer and as an individual with an uncanny capacity to empathize and identify with my thinking. He has captured in the following pages fully and precisely my most subtle feelings and expressions.

Some of you will find this book a real paradox. Before you've finished it, you'll be actually utilizing ESP to perform startling effects. Yet I'll tell you now and explain in detail later that the whole concept of "extrasensory" perception is unnecessary.

I have been an archcritic of many of the claims of so-called psychics and their ilk. Yet I think the darkest day of the great Houdini's life was when, wearying as an escape artist and failing as a magician, he devoted himself to exposing mediums. As you'll learn in the pages to follow, while deceit and fraud exist among those who claim to be explorers of the mind, the facts —as you will see them and experience them—can't be ignored.

Many aspects of parapsychology—ESP, the hypnotic trance, clairvoyance, and such—are long overdue for scientific debunking. Out of their ashes, I believe, will come unprecedented knowledge of man's mental capabilities. This book is but a first step. It is based on skills, mental abilities, that I have devoted my entire life to developing. Since childhood I have utilized them to entertain others, and there is no reason that you cannot do so, too. Some of the effects you will produce, particularly in the beginning, are mere illusions, simple placebos designed to establish an essential relationship between you and your audience. Later you will achieve startling effects that neither you nor I can explain.

Whether you use this book as a guide at your next party or share it with a friend or turn to it alone in the private seclusion of your room, I hope you'll enjoy it for what it is meant to be —a dramatic learning experience, one of amazement, laughter, intrigue, and joy that can best be appreciated in the theater of your mind. The curtain is due to open; I trust that you will never allow it again to close.

ESPecially,
Kreskin

*Kreskin's Fun Way
to Mind Expansion*

ONE

First, a Word . . .

All is miracle. The stupendous order of nature, the revolution of a hundred million worlds around a million suns, the activity of light, the life of animals, all are grand and perpetual miracles.
                                                                        —VOLTAIRE

"Amazing! But how did you *do* it?"

I'm asked that question hundreds of times a year in person and by letter, and not only by those who have seen me perform at a nightclub, college campus, special "concert," or on television. Some of the most curious are well-known celebrities.

My response is always the same: I am not a psychic, an occultist or fortune-teller. I am not a mind reader, medium, or "hypnotist." There is nothing supernatural about anything that I do.

I am a scientist, a researcher in the field of suggestion and "extrasensory" perceptions. I perform what I discover.

About 85 percent of a typical Kreskin "concert," as I call my performances, involves these mental laws, which is why I call myself a mentalist. The remaining 15 percent of each performance is usually devoted to traditional magic.

That's what I've told Johnny Carson, Mike Douglas, Merv Griffin, Phyllis Diller, and countless others. Of course, not everyone is completely satisfied with that answer, for it is, admittedly, vague. I am going to give specific answers now, in these pages, for the first time ever. *I'm going to reveal the basic principles whereby, using the untapped power of your personality, your persuasiveness, and your ability to perceive beyond the ordinary senses, you too can direct and command many startling effects.*

I'll explain in the following chapters how you can duplicate step by step the amazing effects that have held millions and millions across the nation spellbound. I'll tell you how to prepare your mind and body so that you can reach the level of confidence and concentration you'll need to perform these experiments with friends in your own living room. And where possible, I'll explain the mental processes—the so-called "secrets"—that make these experiments in mind power work.

I say "where possible" for a very good reason: the further you progress in developing the extraordinary powers of your mind, the more baffled you will become by your remarkable abilities. I am absolutely convinced there is nothing supernatural involved in this. Someday, hopefully soon, researchers will be able to identify the force that is at play when, for example, I am able to tell a total stranger the number on his Social Security card or predict in advance, in writing, the headline on next week's newspaper.

I can't explain all the effects you will produce after studying this book. Some, as I have mentioned, are simple illusions in the ancient tradition of the magician. Others, particularly those dealing with ESP, are currently beyond complete explanation. Yet you'll be surprised at how far you'll come toward understanding—and using—ESP yourself. The British Society for Psychical Research once proposed that thought perception, or mind reading, is accomplished by extreme sensitivity to the slightest details and the slightest changes in the person whose thoughts are being received—for example, a change in the muscles of the face, even the smell of the body. I do believe that I recognize physical characteristics that telegraph the thought that produced them. But I also believe there's a great deal more to ESP, although I don't know what, precisely. And maybe I *shouldn't* know. As my former colleague Dr. Harold Hanson said, "It's better you don't know everything that's happening when you're presenting your program, because, obviously, at some point in your show you're harnessing something more than you'd be able to if you were self-conscious of what's happening."

I agree with that. It's not necessary to understand why things work as they do. In fact, trying to understand them, to reduce them to a formula, interferes with the smooth functioning of extrasensory processes. The intellect rears itself like a wall in front of these natural intuitive senses.

It's the same with emotions. Suppose, for example, you awaken one morning feeling particularly happy, but since you are an intellectual person, you think, "Now, why on earth am I happy? I don't have enough money to pay the bills, my kids need braces, the car just failed inspection, and income taxes are due in a month." Chances are, that wall of intellectual detail will quickly and efficiently separate you from your happy emotion.

It will do the same in your pursuit of the deeper uses of your "extra" senses if you insist on understanding how you are able to produce every effect.

Don't misunderstand—I'm not at all against intellectualism, and frankly, I consider myself an intellect in my field. I am simply saying—in fact, I am insisting—that truth comes in various forms and that the intellect is capable of revealing only one form of truth. We cannot understand emotional truth through the intellect. In fact, I have never heard an intellectually satisfying definition of love; although I have seen examples of happiness, I have never had happiness convincingly explained to me. The intellect fails us there, for that is the realm of the emotions, and the intellect cannot speak emotional truths. Nor can we expect to understand, at least for now, all extrasensory truths, for they are the domain of experience. We *feel* them, we watch them work, and that is how we know they are true.

But understand this: there is nothing supernatural, metaphysical, or occult about this. Phyllis Diller once jokingly said, "Kreskin is a male witch and should be burned at the stake!" —and others have called me a psychic, a medium, and even a saint. The fact is that I am like most people, except that I've trained my mind to respond hypersensitively to the subtle senses that most people ignore.

I do nothing that any ten-year-old child couldn't do if he had thirty years' experience.

This book will do more than make you the life of the party. I have known thousands of people who, by applying the methods used in these mind games, have become more compelling in conversation, more successful professionally, more popular socially. Others have learned to relax and sleep, to shrug away tensions, to make wise, future-oriented decisions—the list is virtually endless.

I'll help you to find these practical benefits every step of the way, so that you'll learn not only how to master amazing effects and the principles behind them but also how to apply those principles to your everyday life. Just one example: while learning how to plant a suggestion in another person's mind, you will discover how to awaken each morning without an alarm clock, feel more energetic, and solve problems that you thought were beyond you.

Now, let's begin this adventure together, this journey into ourselves and our friends, and along the way you will discover things about people you probably never imagined—and you might come to know more about yourself as well.

TWO

Prepare to Concentrate

The typical mind is a floodlight; the concentrated mind is a laser.

It seems almost a basic law of nature that every large party includes at least one skeptic. When this happens, you might try this entertaining means of making a convert. Begin by saying:

"No doubt you have a very strong mind. How long does it take you to lower your pulse by ten percent?"

Chances are, the question will astonish him. Everyone knows the pulse, or heartbeat, is an involuntary process like digestion, peristalsis (contractions of the intestines), and other metabolic processes. Before the skeptic dismisses you as tipsy, ask:

"You mean you've *never* decreased your heart rate by an act of will? Certainly you can decrease your pulse by ten beats a minute—or at least *five?*"

Now, the doubter will certainly ask if you can do it yourself.
Say:

"Certainly. Anyone can. And I promise I will—later."
Then, lay on the challenge: "All right, why not show everyone
how easy it is?"

You've put him on the spot. Have him take a comfortable
seat and select a man from the group to monitor the subject's
pulse. Explain at considerable length and with assurance:

"Now, we're going to let you relax for a few minutes so that
we can establish your resting pulse rate. Try to relax. The next
few minutes don't count."

Instruct the monitor to adjust his wristwatch so that he can
see the sweep second hand and to locate the subject's pulse.
Tell him—privately, if possible—to ignore the first minute but
to count the pulse for the second and third minutes without
making it obvious.

While the pulse is being taken, talk in a calm, relaxed manner about a tranquil subject that will divert the subject's attention from the test. Your intent is to overcome his natural ap-
prehension, which would increase pulse rate.

When the monitor announces the pulse rate, say:

"That's pretty low for this particular test because of the
excitability factor. I don't know how much lower you can get
it—although I've seen people with *real* willpower do surpris-
ingly well." Challenge the subject with a smile. Ask him:

"Are you ready to concentrate on lowering your pulse?"

Instruct the monitor to repeat the pulse-taking process
while you casually discuss the dynamics of heart rate: "When
a rabbit sees a stalking bloodhound, its heart might surge to a
couple of hundred beats per minute, which sends oxygen-rich
red blood gushing through its arteries to nourish every cell of
its body." Use vivid action words to explain that fear, anxiety,
pain, and physical exercise all speed up the heart rate. "But a
rabbit hasn't the brain or will of our subject who, merely by
concentration, can slow his heartbeat by ten beats per minute."

What you're saying is entirely correct—but your subject is

concentrating on the *wrong things.* You're directing his thoughts to the violent color of blood, to the thumping of his heart, to the possibility of failure and the embarrassment it would entail. And when the monitor announces the pulse rate, everyone will find that it has not only failed to decline—but it has actually increased.

The skeptic will immediately insist that the pulse rate cannot be reduced by willpower. And you'll proceed to prove otherwise. This chapter will show you how.

One of the teachers I had in junior high school when I was growing up in Caldwell, New Jersey, repeated a favorite accusation so many times that, in all justice, it should be carved on her tombstone. Several times a day she declared, "You're not concentrating!"

In my case, at least, she was mistaken. The one thing I did well as a child was to concentrate. In fact, it was this total concentration on a thirteen-year-old classmate named Lisa that led to the teacher's occasional outbursts.

Virtually all living creatures have the capacity to "concentrate," or focus attention. Watch a cat concentrate on a bird in an open field, eyes and ears focused utterly on its prey, every muscle rigid, awaiting the moment when the bird begins to concentrate on extracting a worm and neglects its own safety.

Even houseflies "concentrate," and you can prove it to yourself the next time one lands on your arm. If you try to swat it quickly, chances are you'll miss. Wait until the insect has found an appetizing portion of your anatomy and begins concentrating on dinner, brushing its hind legs together. Then, *whack!*

Children have a wonderful capacity to concentrate, as all parents know. Call Joey for dinner when he's engrossed in play in the next room, and he simply won't hear you. Talk to him while he's concentrating on a television program and he won't even know you're in the room.

Every day we see examples of supreme concentration. In baseball, hitters concentrate so intently on a ball's progress from pitcher to home plate that in a fraction of a second they coordinate countless nerve impulses to bring a bat in contact with a hundred-mile-per-hour ball. When concentration wanders, the batter is left flailing the air.

We watch a field goal kicker as he closes his mind to sixty thousand screaming fans, the score, the other players, and focuses his entire existence on putting the ball through the uprights. One kicker, Ray Wersching, with the San Francisco 49ers, concentrates so deeply on "reliving" the physical coordination of his perfect kicks that, from the moment he steps on the field, he refuses to even *look* at the goalposts. The yard markers tell him how long the kick must be, and the player holding the ball indicates the direction. Wersching's job, as he sees it, is to concentrate on executing a perfect kick. Getting through the goalposts is the *ball's* job, and Wersching refuses to weaken his concentration by worrying about that.

Next time you watch a great dramatic performer like Ingrid Bergman, Maureen Stapleton, or Alec Guinness in a motion picture, try to imagine what's *really* happening: Half a dozen cameramen, directors and their assistants, prop and costume people, stage and floor managers, technical consultants, other performers all milling around a tiny set with cardboard walls in a big, dingy building not unlike an airplane hangar. Cold white lights glare on the actors; microphones dangle above them. Yet, when the director yells, "Action!" a miracle of concentration unfolds.

The performers become oblivious to the confusion around them. So deep is their concentration that they literally *become* the characters they portray. The circumstances of the script become *their* circumstances, and the passions they reveal are the genuine passions that grow out of their concentration.

In all the manifestations of illusion and mind power that we will discuss hereafter, from ESP to suggestion, *concentration is the key.* I suspect that to a great extent the gift of telepathy is the capacity for profound concentration. My performances demand nonstop concentration, beginning an hour before showtime, and the effort is so exhausting that I lose as much as three pounds during a three-hour concert and must eat five meals a day to regain the weight.

One reason for the great energy output is that I must concentrate on *many* details with *equal* intensity at the *same* time. Here's what I mean:

Some years ago, I was challenged to duplicate an escape that Houdini had made famous. I'm a mentalist, not an escape artist, but the idea was challenging and so I practiced for several months. It was to be done on live television and before an audience, and I wanted to be certain I could do it within a very restricted time limit.

The night of the performance I discovered that I'd failed to take into consideration several factors. One was the heat. I'd never rehearsed under thousands of watts of glaring spotlights, and there on the stage, with my hands cuffed behind my back, cramped into a fetal position in a small canvas sack that was sealed with a metal bar and padlocks, the heat quickly became almost suffocating. It came close to wrecking my concentration.

A second problem was that the police officer who volunteered to handcuff me had done it with a vengeance. He'd practically cut off the circulation, and by the time I had slipped free of the handcuffs my wrists were bloody. Pain, I assure you, threatens concentration.

Finally, the presence of the audience, especially those who doubted that I would succeed and the few (there are always a few) who actually hoped that I would fail, was a distracting factor. Negative feelings in an audience affect me like one violinist playing off-key in a large orchestra.

The escape was a success, but when the curtain was pulled aside, the audience saw a Kreskin that must have resembled a half-drowned mouse. My clothes were soaked with sweat, my wrists injured, and my hair disheveled. And when we went to a commercial break, I simply sat on the floor, stunned.

The physical challenge explains only a part of the exhaustion I felt. A great deal was caused by the concentration required. Yet I had to continue to concentrate for at least an hour more, until the program was over. I concentrate on the "messages" various members of the audience are sending. Someone is very happy, fondling a ring. The color red. A dress. Somewhere in the audience, I realize, a woman wearing a red dress has just become engaged or married.

The color blue. Sky, water. Someone is looking forward to an ocean voyage. I visualize the beard. He's thinking about the boat. It has two sails.

I file these messages away for use later in the concert.

I'm also concentrating on traditional sensory input, particularly sights and sounds. Supernormal awareness of sensory stimuli is known as hyperesthesia, of which I'll have much more to say later. This highly developed ability to concentrate on our ordinary senses might actually explain much telepathic communication.

For example, some years ago, when I was performing at the Las Vegas Hilton, I heard a soft, continuous clicking in the audience. It wasn't the tinkling of coins, or the dull sound of wood, but the clacking of plastic gaming chips. Finally, when the noise—for it became that to me—threatened to intrude on my overall concentration, I stopped, walked to the edge of the stage, and addressed a man in the third row who was playing with the chips in his pocket.

"Your mind is on placing a bet. You feel lucky. Perhaps you should act on it."

He left immediately. I don't know whether he won or lost, but I know my concentration improved—and the audience thought I'd read his mind.

It was at the Embers Club in Indianapolis that I decided some years ago to find out just how sensitive my hearing really was. Bob Kaytes, maitre d', cooperated. Every night for a week, Bob or a staff member dropped an object to the floor during a performance, and if the crowd was relatively quiet, making no more than the usual sounds of breathing, glasses clinking, and soft murmuring, I could detect the sound.

Ultimately, I found that through concentration I could actually detect the sound of a needle dropping to the floor. Since then, I've done the same in large auditoriums—but I confess I haven't a chance if the floor is carpeted.

And now to one of the most important lessons you'll learn in these pages—my personal method of achieving intense concentration. Don't just read this chapter—*practice* it. Then, keep *on* practicing it. And all the rest will fall into place.

STEP ONE: CLEAR THE LANDSCAPE

Sometimes I really enjoy cranking up the Mercedes and driving to a distant city where I'll perform. I prefer it to flying if the distance isn't too great and the directions are simple.

What I *don't* like is confusion. The Baltimore Beltway is a perfect example—six-lane expressways, traffic merging and exiting left and right, speeding trucks blocking the road signs. During my first experience on that road, driving from Harrisburg to Washington, DC, I followed what I thought was the main highway only to discover I had entered another expressway and was heading toward New York City.

The same thing can happen with thoughts. In the clutter of our lives the mental landscape gets confusing. Ideas, problems, decisions, come and go from every direction. Distractions lurk everywhere, and our minds continually drift off in the wrong direction.

The first step in concentration is to clear the landscape.

Letting the Body Go

You've probably heard the term *holism*. Dorland's Illustrated Medical Dictionary defines it as "the conception of man as a functioning whole." It means that the body and mind are not separate entities, but the body in some ways is actually a part of the mind, and vice versa. Cold, damp weather makes us emotionally moody because our bodies are uncomfortable. On the other hand, our emotional problems can cause serious physical illness, including intolerable pain. These are called psychosomatic or body-mind ailments—but even that term implies two distinct entities.

Failure to recognize the oneness of body/mind is probably the major reason that some people can't relax completely. Tension in the body is tension in the mind. You can't sleep if your muscles are tense, and you can't concentrate.

For that reason—to relax the muscles of my body—I jog a couple of miles every morning. And before every TV show or concert I take a brisk one-mile walk. That walk is as important as any other aspect of my preparation. I can actually *feel* the tension subsiding. It usually begins in the muscles around my neck and shoulders. Then the liquid, flowing feeling seeps into those stubborn back muscles. My arms begin to feel more limp, and my legs move with an easy, flowing rhythm.

Once the body is relaxed, I can detach myself from distractions and build up an attitude of deep introspection. Frankly, I don't know how I'd survive had I not mastered the art of relaxing, for the schedule can be torturous. In 1978, the last year I kept such records, I presented 613 performances around the world. In a four-month period that year I flew an average of twenty-three flights every ten days, making several connections with only seconds to spare, my luggage often two or three flights behind. (The fine art of luggage-losing has been perfected by some airlines.)

The rigors of such a schedule have been the downfall of many great performers. A well-known comedian once told me, "I've cut my bookings in half—I just can't stand the pressure." An expensive psychiatrist had tried to help him relax his mind, but it didn't work.

I wasn't surprised to hear that. *Relaxation—clearing the mental landscape—starts with the body.*

The four primary muscle tension groups of the body are the legs, abdomen, back, and neck/shoulders. And next to an hour-long walk or twenty-minute jog, the best way to relax them is through stretch exercises.

Sitting Toe Touch

Sitting on the floor with your legs outstretched, feet together, reach for your toes. If you aren't very flexible, you probably won't be able to do this at first. Don't strain, just reach. After about a minute, those stubborn, tense muscles in your back and lower calf will begin to relax. As they do, lean farther forward. If you're particularly stiff, you won't reach your toes the first day, perhaps not the second.

When you do, you're halfway to the final goal, which is to touch your forehead to your knees. Long before that you will feel the benefits of stretching and relaxing those back, shoulder, and leg muscles.

Back Bend

Start in a kneeling position. Slowly and carefully lean back. The object is to touch the back of your head to the floor. This must be done carefully and cautiously, for the quadriceps (upper thigh muscles) of most people are not used to being stretched, and a fast movement can tear them. This exercise is wonderful for stretching thigh muscles and those of the chest, neck, and abdomen.

Head Rotation

The most obvious sites of tension in most people are the muscles of the shoulder and back that extend into the neck. We just don't give these muscles much exercise, and the result is that when they grow tight with tension they remain that way. The best exercise for stretching and relaxing them is the old-fashioned head roll.

Drop your head sideways toward your left shoulder. (Unless you're more flexible than most, your head won't touch the shoulder.) Let it droop there, allowing the muscle to stretch.

Roll your head back, slowly and gently, careful not to tear

tight muscles. After a stretching period, roll it over the right shoulder and pause. Finally, let it hang forward.

Repeat the exercise five times, then reverse the direction.

Progressive Relaxation

When you've attained flexibility in the major muscle groups, the next step is progressive physical relaxation. It's the most effective method of muscle relaxation I know, yet it takes only a few minutes.

Progressive relaxation is based on the simple fact that you can't consciously relax a muscle unless you're consciously aware that it's tense. When you *feel* the tension in the muscle, you can deliberately relax it.

Make your hand into a fist. Clench the fist for three seconds, then slowly relax it and let your hand and arm go limp. Repeat it twice, then do it twice with the other hand.

That exercise was introductory only, to give you an idea of what we'll be doing with all the major muscles of your body. Now, close your eyes. Concentrate on the muscles of your forehead, tightening them as much as you can. Don't cheat—make them *really* tight. Maintain the tension for three seconds, then let those muscles relax.

Move on to your jaw muscles, then your neck, shoulders, arms, chest, torso, buttocks, legs, feet.

If you don't feel a dramatic release of tension as you relax the muscles, repeat the exercise—and continue the repetitions, concentrating on both the tension and relaxation, until the muscles do dramatically relax.

And you *will* relax. Much of the muscle tension we endure results from our not being consciously aware of the tension. Many of us go through each day with our muscles unconsciously contracted in preparation for battle, but since most of our enemies in modern life are emotional and psychological, we never get the opportunity to use those muscles and then relax them. Instead, they're in a chronic state of tension, and only by exaggerating that tension can we become aware of it and allow them to relax.

Letting the Mind Go

Now that you've learned to relax your body in a few brief minutes, you're ready for deep mental relaxation. Start by getting comfortable—sitting in a soft chair or lying down. Avoid crossing legs or arms or putting your body in a position in which the circulation will be impaired.

1. Can you recall a time and place of perfect serenity? Most of us can if we try—gazing up at the stars on a warm summer night, lying on a beach while the waves splash a few feet away, resting near the trunk of a tall tree in a towering forest. Perhaps you can recall being a child in your mother's comforting arms, falling asleep in her lap.

Whatever that scene of perfect peace, recall it now.

This scene will become the passkey to deep and rapid relaxation for you, so it's worth your trouble to spend time selecting the most effective one you can. Or if you have a good imagination, you might wish to create your *ideal* scene, one that holds even deeper tranquillity than you've ever known—drifting on a rolling sea, lounging in a candlelit room where you hear only quiet music.

Now, *without effort, without engaging your will,* allow that scene to grow clear in your mind. Please note that I'm using a *passive* construction here—allow it to happen to you. Don't try to force the scene or you'll be working your mind instead of relaxing it.

Allow yourself to dissolve into the scene. See the colors. Smell the pine needles. Listen to the waves or crackling fire or music. Feel the sand or your mother's arms or the carpet or the earth beneath you.

With practice you'll be able to reach that special place in your mind in thirty seconds to a minute, and once there, the outside world won't distract you from it.

2. Now you're ready to empty your mind completely. Think of a passive, tranquil color. Light blue and pale green work best for me. Perhaps you will prefer gray or a soft beige. Allow the vision of your tranquil place to dissolve slowly in the color until there is nothing . . . nothing but that hue in your mind.

3. Slowly inhale deeply, then let the air flow out until your diaphragm is completely relaxed. Repeat two more times, and when you exhale for the third time, allow your entire mind and body to go completely limp.

You're now totally relaxed. You've cleared the landscape of the distracting traffic, junctions, merging lanes, and exit ramps. You're ready to concentrate, to re-create the one highway along which you want your mind to travel.

But before we go on, let me show you what you've *already* achieved. First, you've come to grips with the everyday stress that is part and parcel of modern society. While stress is essential to all forms of life, and some people flourish under it, there is no question that millions die every year from the high blood pressure, heart disease, and ulcers that are the byproducts of our stressful life-styles.

To combat stress with alcohol, tranquilizers, and other drugs seems to be on the order of treating a headache by dashing your skull against a brick wall. The solution is likely to be more destructive than the problem. Every time I step out on a stage I face three hours of exhausting, withering stress, but I have not once taken a pill or a drink to relax. In fact, my staple beverage is grapefruit juice, and an occasional cup of tea.

After a couple of weeks of practice with the relaxation technique, you'll be able to shed pressures in from two to five minutes, take a thoroughly restful vacation in the most tranquil environment you know, and return with enthusiasm and alertness, unimpaired by drugs or alcohol.

Some people reach a point in total relaxation where they feel completely detached from their bodies. In fact, I believe that this sensation of disembodiment through relaxation has caused some people to imagine that they have actually separated from their bodies, or had what is known as an out-of-body expe-

rience. I consider the OBE a sincere misunderstanding, a fig-
ment of the imagination. If nothing else, it's a beneficial
minivacation—and the price is right.

What else can total relaxation do? A young college student
sits facing a TV-like screen. From the metal cuffs around his
arms, wires extend to a shiny box with gauges and knobs. Dr.
Neal Miller of Rockefeller University in New York stands by,
along with a few associates. The room is silent; the young man
totally relaxed.

After a few moments the machine with the gauges and
knobs makes a bleeping sound. The dark screen brightens to
reveal a dazzling landscape, a brief reward for the young man
who has somehow achieved what has long been considered
impossible: he has lowered his blood pressure, slowed his heart
rate and even reduced the electrical activity of his brain,
achieving the conscious control of involuntary body functions
after achieving complete relaxation.

Serious practitioners of yoga have accomplished "visceral
learning" for thousands of years, and a few masters have
slowed their metabolic rates so dramatically that they have
survived burial in a coffin for several days—the ultimate in
total relaxation.

Personally, I have never tried being buried in a coffin—it's
just not among my top ten favorite ways to spend a weekend.
But in a matter of minutes I can lower my pulse from the
normal seventy-two beats per minute to between fifteen and
eighteen as I completely relax.

And at that party I described in the beginning, you too will
decrease your heart rate by at least ten beats a minute. During
the first, or threshold, pulse measure, think of something emotionally stimulating. Then request silence, spend thirty seconds
establishing your tranquil scene and another thirty seconds
allowing it to dissolve to clear the landscape. Stay there, in the
relaxed world of quiet color, allowing everything to slip away,
oblivious of the time, the guests, the room.

Only when the guests announce in amazement that you've
succeeded will you return.

IMAGE INTEGRATION

I do not exaggerate the importance of the remainder of this chapter when I say it is the key to all that you wish to accomplish through reading this book. Virtually every effect, from simple illusion to "foretelling" the future and receiving information telepathically, will require both a higher degree and a higher quality of concentration than most people ever demand of themselves.

Yet effective concentration doesn't require superior intelligence. Ordinary people can accomplish it with ease once they understand the objective and technique.

I call my approach to concentration *image integration,* and for good reason: we enhance our concentration not by an act of will (remember the skeptic whose willpower only served to defeat him?) but by bringing together as many sensory "images" as possible into a single penetrating focal point of thought.

If that sounds confusing, let me put it this way. One night your neighbor hears a stirring on the lawn. He turns on an outdoor floodlight, but because the rabbit that prompted his concern remains motionless, the neighbor is unable to distinguish it from all the equally lighted surroundings.

You, on the other hand, have money to burn. You like to watch rabbits on your lawn. So you've installed a sensitive electronic grid beneath the grass. Now every time a rabbit hops on the grid, half a dozen spotlights blink on, each trained directly on the same spot. The surrounding lawn is in total darkness, but the rabbit is bathed in light from every angle.

Preposterous as the analogy is, it makes the point. Most people concentrate in floodlight fashion—they're unable to eliminate the peripheral and focus on the essential.

When you're done reading and practicing this chapter, you'll concentrate differently. Just as the rabbit, not you, triggered the lighting on your lawn, so the subject on which you need to concentrate will trigger the images that will focus your full attention, while leaving the surrounding landscape in darkness.

When I speak of "images," I'm talking about those of the senses: sight, sound, smell, taste, and touch. There are other senses, perhaps, the "extra" senses of ESP. But I've never seen evidence that they're involved in concentration—and I suspect that at least some of the extra senses are really unusual applications of the five basic senses.

Prepare to Concentrate

I was in Reno, Nevada, in 1977, when a University of Nevada coed was murdered. The police had four eyewitnesses, but each had only a moment to glance at the killer as they passed in a moving car. None could give a useful description.

The authorities asked me to help. I felt that if I could get each witness to concentrate, to exclude all the peripheral sights and sounds and to zoom in, so to speak, on the killer's face, there might be a chance that at least one could give a clear description. In fact, three of the four had such vivid recall that they described the suspect in precisely the same way and detail.

Here's the exercise I led them through. It is the exercise you must practice regularly—once or twice daily if possible—for at least 20 minutes.

Step One. Follow the total relaxation techniques until your mind is empty, its landscape a soft and passive shade of green, blue, or gray throughout.

Step Two. Focus on a preselected scene or object, one that you can associate with each of the five familiar senses—but *not* the scene you use for total relaxation.

Include movement in the scene if possible. In the next chapter I'll show you how vivid is our recall of that sense. I once knew a fellow so open to the suggestion of movement that we could blindfold him, place him on a rug, tell him that the rug was being pulled out from under him and watch him react. He would "feel" the movement, adjust his balance to compensate and fall forward—where we would be waiting to catch him.

Don't force the scene or object—allow it to come to you.

Let's assume you've chosen an orange. Against the void of landscape, you'll see the form take shape. The skin will glisten. Is there a drop of moisture on it? The orange color is rich and warm, the skin punctuated with pores. Is there a blue produce stamp on the side? Is the fruit perfectly round?

You'll smell the tangy aroma. It might make your mouth water. You'll feel the skin, so different from an apple's, rough and rubbery. Toss it in the air. Feel the weight of it as it lands in your hand.

Feel it, open it. Apples go *crack* when the halves are pulled apart. The orange makes more of a squish sound.

The smell is richer now. Taste it. It tastes like it smells, doesn't it—tangy, sweet?

You can follow the same procedures with a scene, incorporating the motion of a moving car, your own arms and legs pumping while you walk. A scene allows for much more input, and if you give yourself just a few extra minutes—right now—you can have an experience that will perhaps amaze you.

Be patient as your scene unfolds. Some people keep a mental checklist in the corner of their minds, and as each sensory experience occurs they mark it off and go on to the next. Of course there's some benefit even to that, but they will remain forever amateurs in the art of image integration. You're not out to keep score but to have a unique experience in concentration.

Observe what's happening in the scene. Someone's cooking steaks on an outside grill and *of course* you can smell it. *Certainly* you can hear the sizzling fat as it falls on the charcoal. Your mouth waters with the taste you'll experience.

There are sounds everywhere—from the volleyball players, the street, the birds. As you open yourself to sensory imagery, it comes from everywhere. You're filling up with it to overflowing. You can even "zoom in" on details, recognizing things you hadn't noticed when you were actually there before. You aren't remembering—you're *reliving* the scene.

Of course, that's precisely how I enabled the Reno murder witnesses to describe the killer, although none of them even realized they had seen him at first. Without using polygraphs, truth serums, or "hypnosis," I used imagery integration to help them concentrate on every detail of the experience. So vivid was their recall that three out of four were able to relive the scene in their minds and take the time to study the mental picture and describe the man they saw in it. The descriptions were virtually identical.

It takes no special talent, no rehearsal. And the effect can be dramatic.

Now you know how to relax and to concentrate—the bed-rock on which all the rest is built. From this point on I won't refer to either of these subjects except when an unusual degree of concentration is required. I'll say only this before we go on to the next chapter: if you find yourself failing repeatedly in the effects that follow, return to this chapter and master it before going on.

THREE

The Art of Illusion

Even the most hardened skeptic believes what his senses tell him —but the senses are easily deceived.

The male peacock, when threatened, transforms itself from a rather drab and awkwardly shaped creature into a glorious jewel of iridescence. That's how we humans see the displaying peacock, but to a prowling dog there's nothing glorious about that transformation. In fact, it's downright scary.

Before the dog's very eyes the peacock has grown huge. It towers over the dog—no longer just one helpless bird but now a dozen huge, brilliant, unblinking eyes confronting the animal. The bird screeches, steps closer, the eyes threatening— and almost invariably the dog retreats.

It's an illusion, of course—"an erroneous perception of reality," as the dictionary defines the word. The peacock is relatively defenseless against the dog, but the dog has seen with his own eyes the great size and fearlessness of the peacock, and trusting his senses, he has drawn the rational conclusion.

Nature abounds with illusion. Carnivorous plants use it to lure the insects on which they dine. Large fish use it to lure small ones. Other fish enlarge themselves when danger approaches, or they have evolved into species with large, frightening heads, or they have bright violent colors—all to give the illusion of viciousness.

Illusion is universal in everyday human affairs as well. The citizens of militantly Communist countries regularly hear with their own ears and read with their own eyes the "fact" that the United States is a war-hungry nation, and countless millions have come to believe the illusion.

Americans, too, swallow illusions. When was the last time you rinsed your mouth so you'd have kissing-sweet breath, or used a perfume or cologne to help you meet someone handsome or beautiful at the beach, or bought a computer so you'd be successful in business? Most advertising depends for its success on persuading you to accept a subtle illusion: that you too can be like the person using the product in the ad or commercial. Few people buy a product because they *consciously* accept that illusion. Yet they have seen people they admire—celebrities, athletes, and such—using the product, and they have unconsciously bought the erroneous conclusion the commercial implied.

The mentalist, too, uses illusion. I devote a significant portion of every concert exclusively to it, and it is *absolutely crucial* to the audience conditioning that makes possible the later telepathic effects.

Your *first* challenge as an entertainer, whether on stage or at a party, will be to establish what literary people call *suspension of disbelief.* Every time we see a play or a film or read a novel, our intellect tells us none of it is real. Yet to enjoy the experience, we must allow ourselves to believe that it is. We put our critical faculties on the shelf.

The mentalist who attempts to demonstrate telepathy and other forms of ESP faces an obstacle that the novelist needn't deal with: A reader wouldn't pick up the book in the first place unless he was ready to believe in it, but people *will* show up in the mentalist's audience who project the thought, loud and clear, "I don't believe any of this. I *dare* you to convince me."

They're like the patient in the dental chair who responds to the dentist's assurances about the whirring drill with "Oh sure, *sure* it won't hurt!"

Well, when I was a child, I was fortunate enough to have a very patient dentist who took the time to touch that low-speed drill first to his finger and then to mine before approaching my teeth with it. He convinced me that the drill was harmless and that it couldn't hurt (which, thank God, it didn't). It was an illusion, of course, but an effective one that earned my cooperation in the serious work at hand.

The illusion segment of my performances serve just that purpose: to prepare the audience to cooperate with the serious work at hand. You should do the same with the illusions in this chapter. As you learn to execute these effects smoothly and confidently, you'll actually *sense* your friends' conversion from skeptics to believers.

I can hardly exaggerate the importance of a cooperative attitude. *You cannot achieve ESP effects until your subjects are on your side.* I learned that the hard—and expensive—way some years ago when I performed at a high school in Connecticut. It was a fund-raising benefit. Half a dozen teachers and about the same number of students wanted to fly to Aspen to go skiing—in spite of the fact that they lived within driving distance of the magnificent slopes of Massachusetts, Maine, and Vermont. So they hired me to perform, and the profits were to go to this educational venture in Aspen.

Several of the teachers who, along with the school psychologist, formed the sponsoring committee, invited me to dinner at one of their homes before the concert, and it was there that I first felt apprehensive. Everyone was very friendly and warm, yet I felt extremely unsettled. I finally left the table. My road manager joined me in the kitchen. The first thing he said was, "Kreskin, what's the matter with you?"

I couldn't tell him then, but later I understood.

I ended the program that night as I usually do, allowing a group of strangers to hide my paycheck anywhere in the auditorium, and finding it. But the people selected by the committee were not strangers at all; they were those who had been at the dinner with me earlier in the evening. I understood immediately why I had been troubled during the dinner: these people had been thinking and perhaps planning about the final part of the evening, and in spite of the outward friendliness, there had been an undercurrent of hostility.

I now realize that it was foolhardy and unprofessional of me to accept the check-hiding committee that was offered—it's my policy to insist on total strangers. Yet I agreed and went through with the test. I believe I must have covered every square inch of that auditorium in my mind, and I kept returning to the back door, finally pounding it with my fist in utter frustration—but I knew the check couldn't be outside, for the rules stipulated that it had to be within the auditorium.

Finally, furious, feeling an enormous amount of hostility, I turned to one of the subjects, catching him off guard, and demanded, *"Are you really thinking of where it's hidden?"* and he blurted, "No, Kreskin—we all agreed to think of the wrong place."

Hundreds of people in the audience gasped.

I've never been paid for that evening, and I imagine my uncollected fee helped to keep the Aspen educational experience going for perhaps an extra week. I can overcome a great deal of static and interference in receiving thoughts from others, but when there is hostility or deliberate attempt to deceive, I'm virtually helpless.

There are two postscripts to that story, incidentally. The first is that the committee members had agreed to think—actually to envision—the check as lying on the ground outside of the auditorium door. That's why I kept returning to the door in frustration. The second is that several members of the audience, hearing the committee member admit to deceiving me, wrote letters to the local newspaper. It was not a very large town, and these letters, with accompanying articles, made the front page. An editorial declared that deceit in the name of education was a disgrace to the town. Reporters interviewed me by telephone, the Board of Education called a special press conference to explain its side of the story, and the psychologist, who apparently had been instrumental in the entire matter, dropped out of sight for two weeks.

A trusting, believing relationship is essential to any "extrasensory" communication you hope to establish with your audience. I'll return to this matter in some detail later, but for now let me simply say that there might actually be a neurochemistry of belief, a hormonal factor that affects the brain, and perhaps the rest of the body as well, in a way that a skeptic does not experience. People in all walks of life have seen the dramatic effects of belief:

• Athletes of ordinary ability whose *belief* in themselves make them champions.

• Patients diagnosed as terminally ill who, *believing* they would recover, did just that.

• The literally millions who, *believing* in what we commonly call ESP, have had "extrasensory" experiences.

Two thousand years ago Jesus said that even the tiniest grain of pure faith could move mountains. We still can't demonstrate why it is so, yet history might be defined as a chronicle of that truth.

To build belief, to suspend doubt, master and use the following illusions.

PUNCH THE POTATO

Ask the host for a raw potato and a few ordinary paper drinking straws—*not* plastic ones. (To be on the safe side, I usually bring a few straws with me.) Ask for a volunteer, and say:

"Pick up any one of the straws and hold it at the upper end.

Concentrate on making it hard, as hard as metal. When you've willed it into hardness, jab the lower end through the potato."

The straw will crumble on impact, of course.

Ask the volunteer to return to his seat and select another straw. Say:

"Are you sure you didn't concentrate on hardening the *potato?* It's the lower tip of the straw, which comes in contact with the potato, that must be hardened. Let's all concentrate on it together."

After a few seconds of silence say:

"Now!"

To everyone's astonishment, you drive the straw straight through the potato.

While everyone was listening to your words and concentrating on the lower tip of the straw, you were casually bending the upper tip over on itself and pinching it tightly closed so that no air could escape. Now, when you give the straw a straight, hard jab, the cylinder can't cave in—it's filled with a column of air that becomes more compressed as the straw penetrates the potato.

Straighten the straw, crumbling it a bit to hide the folded line, and pass it around for examination. If anyone comments that the top part of the straw is wrinkled, simply explain that you were not concentrating on hardening the *whole* straw.

MATCHED THOUGHT

This effect will do more to build your own sense of confidence than will any other illusion I can think of—and justifiably so, for it's so simple and obvious that its success depends on you alone.

Lay a nickel, a dime, and a penny on the table. Take another nickel from your pocket, allowing no one to see it, and hold it in your hand. Say:

"The coin in my hand matches one of these on the table. I'll guide your thoughts in selecting the matching coin."

In a rapid series of instructions, which you have *rehearsed thoroughly,* you do just that. Let's assume your friend picks the penny. Say:

"Good! Now, take a second coin."

He takes the dime. Say:

"Wonderful. Do you see what coin you've left?" He'll tell you, of course, that it's the nickel. You open your hand to show the matching nickel.

OR

He'll pick up the dime and the nickel. Extend your empty hand toward him and say:

"Good, now think about your choice. Try to concentrate. Give me one of those coins." If he gives you the nickel, exclaim, "Wonderful! You've done it. You've matched the coin!" Reveal the nickel you have held all along.

If he chooses to keep the nickel say:

"Extend your fist with the coin in it. Now open your fist." You do the same.

"We've matched thoughts and chosen the same coin."

And of course if he picks the nickel first, perhaps you really *have* matched thoughts! Obviously, you should avoid attempting this effect twice with the same audience.

MAGICIAN'S CHOICE

This effect, like *Matched Thought,* will succeed only as you *control the direction of your audience's thoughts.* In mind games that's the most important single lesson you can learn. So practice these two illusions until you can confidently and effectively accomplish them.

Pick a card out of a deck, glance at it, and place it face down on the table. Announce to your audience:

"I'm going to project into your thoughts the name of the card on the table. Please concentrate on the card."

After a few seconds ask the subject to name one color, either black or red.

Let's assume the card on the table is the four of clubs. If the subject chooses black, go on to the next question. If he chooses red, say:

"Good, you've chosen to discard red, so black is the color we're left with. Do you choose clubs or spades?"

Again, if the subject chooses clubs, go with it. If he says spades, smile brightly and announce:

"You're doing very well, better than most. You wish to discard the spades, which leaves us with clubs. Now choose picture cards or number cards."

The procedure continues. Let's assume the subject chooses the number cards. Immediately say, "All right, the numbers run from ace to ten. Choose ace through five, or six through ten."

Continue this process of elimination until you're down to three cards. Ask him to pick one of the three.

If he picks the four, he has read your thoughts.

If he picks another, eliminate that card and ask him to pick again. If he chooses the four, he has read your thoughts.

If he still misses the four, eliminate the card he has picked and ask what he's left with. When he announces it, he has read your thoughts.

Casually turn the card over and watch his amazement.

THE SPIRIT TOUCH

Ask your subject to sit in a chair, his head back against a wall so that he can be certain no one is behind him. Bring the forefingers of each hand close to his eyes and say:

"You're going to close your eyes and I'm going to place my fingers against them so that, through the power of my concentration, you'll be able to call up a spirit from the past. It'll take only a few seconds, and the spirit will give you some sign of its presence. Now close your eyes and just relax. Keep them closed until I withdraw my fingers."

The subject does as instructed, and sure enough, as you urge him to concentrate, he feels a gentle touch on his arm or neck.

You remove your fingers from his eyes, holding them an inch away, and say:

"Open your eyes!" He does, and stares bewildered at your extended forefingers while you calmly ask, "Did anything happen?"—as if you didn't know!

This is how to do it:

The instant your subject closes his eyes, touch his eyelids not with your two forefingers but with the first two fingers of *one* hand. Now all you need to do is to set the mood, the expectancy, leading your subject to concentrate not on your fingers but on the spirit he wishes to call through your concentration.

If you sense resistance, explain that you're having difficulty —his mood isn't right, he isn't concentrating. When you're satisfied that he's in the "spirit" of things, lightly touch a few hairs on the back of his head or brush his shoulder with your free hand.

Quickly bring your free hand toward the subject's eyes— some skeptical subjects will try to open them even though you've instructed them not to. Their first instinct is to pull their head backward, but the wall will prevent that. Withdraw the two fingers and simultaneously position the unused forefinger before the eye it was supposedly covering. Ask the subject to open his eyes.

Although I prefer to perform this effect with no witnesses, an assistant who already understands the mystery can be helpful. The subject will suspect him of being party to the illusion, and instead of looking at your fingers, he will turn to the witness—who remains sitting too far from the subject to have been involved.

The next two illusions are favorites of mine because they're so easy to work, so baffling—and they can keep a stubborn party-goer busy for hours. Each requires a simple prop.

THE SPINNING EGG

Come equipped with a dozen fresh eggs. Gather participants around a table and explain that you're now going to teach them how to spin an egg like a top. Everyone, including you, picks an egg.

Set your egg upright on its large end, holding it between the tips of your thumb and second finger, both pointing downward. Now, as though you're snapping your fingers, give the egg a quick, smooth twist. Your egg spins smoothly until it loses velocity and rolls over.

Removing your egg, invite the others to try. Go around the table giving advice, encouraging. To the person apparently having the most difficult time, say:

"Here, try my egg. Maybe it will bring you luck."

But it won't. Say:

"It's really quite simple. Anyone can do it."

Borrow someone else's egg and, after calling attention to another participant who seems almost to have succeeded, demonstrate again how it's done. Then leave the participants to an evening of frustration—none of them will ever succeed.

The spin itself takes practice, so *be sure to rehearse* beforehand. But the major reason you succeed and they fail is that they're spinning raw eggs and your egg is hard-boiled.

Before the egg spinning begins, place your hard-boiled egg where you will easily find it among the eleven others, and when you invite everyone to take an egg, make sure you get yours first. After your spin, casually substitute your egg for a raw one in your pocket. Then if anyone asks to try your egg, convinced that it's somehow special, you can cheerfully assent. And if no one asks, you can insist that they give yours a try.

When you take a fresh egg from the carton or from one of the participants, simply direct the group's attention to the efforts of another participant, and in that moment switch eggs again.

Some fellow who feels that his manhood is at stake because

he can't match your achievements just might demand to see you do it, and immediately pick up your egg to attempt the effect himself. Don't worry—your accomplishment will almost certainly remain unmatched. As I said earlier, spinning even the hard-boiled egg takes practice, and he's not likely to do it in one or two attempts. Give him those chances, then take back your egg and say:

"Here, let me show you one last time how it's done." Then keep your egg and walk away.

TWIST THE APPLE

Bring a bag of apples to the entertainment area, explain that you're going to give instructions on how to break an apple in half, neatly and cleanly, with your bare hands, and ask for volunteers who would like to try. As the hands go up, reach into the bag and toss apples to the volunteers. While still facing the audience, withdraw from the bag an apple of your own. Explain the technique:

"We're going to split the apple the hard way—not horizontally, but vertically—from the stem through the core. Now, hold the apple upright, place one hand on the left side, and one on the right and *twist.*"

As you explain it, you do it—but chances are nobody will succeed.

You have technique on your side. Your fingers are turned in opposite directions, one thumb up, one down. Twist in opposite directions, as though opening a tight-lidded jar. In that way, when you exert pressure, you're using not merely forearm or wrist muscles but also the powerful muscles of your chest.

But there's more to it than that—you also have a gimmick. When you reached into the bag for your own apple, you found it in a smaller bag originally hidden beneath the apples you threw to the audience. Here's what you must do before showtime:

Push a long, thin needle through the apple at the stem into

and through the core. Using the tough stem as a focal point, move the needle back and forth so that it cuts the apple in half at the core. You needn't cut particularly close to the skin—the apple will break anyway.

As a finale, explain to the frustrated volunteers that *anyone* can do it if he or she can simply concentrate with sufficient intensity. Withdraw another prepared apple from the bag and give it to any young lady of ordinary strength who has *not* volunteered and therefore does not have an apple of her own. Show her the proper way to grip the apple, tell her to hold it in front of her chest and twist the two halves in opposite directions, as though opening a tight-lidded jar.

The apple will snap in half, and the young lady herself will be the most baffled of all.

In accomplishing these illusions, you've been controlling the attention of the participants, directing it where you want it rather than where it would naturally wander. You've been the magnet, and their attention has been the compass needle. Under your influence the needle no longer points to magnetic north, its natural direction, but to wherever you guide it.

Conditioning an audience to surrender its attention to my direction is really the secret of much that I accomplish during a performance. I believe—and I will test my belief one of these days—that I can now so rivet the attention of an audience that at the right moment a band could march across the stage behind me and go unnoticed by the people. It's emphatically *not* mass hypnosis. I'll not undertake a tirade against the entire concept of hypnosis here but reserve that for three chapters hence. I'll simply repeat that one of the great secrets of my work is conditioning the audience to accept the illusions I propose.

It's a skill that can be used in personal relationships as well —I would hope *not* for devious purposes but to win friends, succeed in job interviews, persuade organizations to see the benefits of your proposals, and such.

Now I'm going to tell you how it's done. That doesn't mean

you'll succeed. Success depends on your *sensitivity,* your ability to *apply* what you read, and your own instinct to empathize and interest.

Rapport

Good rapport, as I use the term, means being in tune, or in step. I once knew a contractor who wanted to build a garage onto a house. The zoning law in the small northeastern Pennsylvania community where he operated prohibited any construction within ten feet of the property line, but his plan would have brought the garage to about nine feet. The building permit was routinely rejected. He insisted on a hearing. That too was routine, and often exceptions were granted.

The contractor started his presentation by saying, "This law is idiotic, and those who voted for it are morons." After those heartwarming words, I doubt that the Pope himself could have persuaded the zoning board to grant a variance.

The contractor was out of tune with the board's thinking and feelings. He was out of step with them.

The ideal rapport is a *mirror image* of those you're confronting. Allow them to see their *best selves* in you. If you're talking to someone who's bombastic, be pleasantly bombastic —but not competitive. If the person is shy and soft-spoken, reflect that tone in yourself. Some people have earthy, open natures; others are high-society types. Some have been hurt by life, others have gone through it unscathed. There's a little of everyone else inside each of us, and the challenge is to find what in us is in tune with the other person and reflect it.

Each of us has a particular way of speaking: a cadence, a speed, a vocabulary. Most of us appreciate a particular kind of humor—we don't necessarily laugh at the same jokes that our neighbor does. Being in tune means reflecting these aspects of the other person.

Even your physical presence can enhance or detract from rapport. I'm quick to remove tie and jacket and roll up shirt sleeves the instant I sense that my audience is in a casual mood. Often when I'm with a small group of college students who prefer sitting on the floor, I join them there—towering above them would clearly set me apart. When the relationship is one-to-one, I study the person's gestures. Does he use his hands a lot? I do too. If not, I won't either.

Appreciation

I firmly believe there's much in every person to admire. It's easy for me to spot the special characteristics in people—their talent for decorating, selecting clothes, thinking through problems, raising fine children, even making me feel at ease. And when I recognize something worth complimenting, I compliment.

There's no room for phoniness or deceit in this business of appreciation. There's nothing easier to recognize, at least on the unconscious level, than a compliment that's unwarranted or insincere. If you don't *believe* it, don't *say* it.

On the other hand, when you compliment someone for what he already appreciates in himself, you're reflecting not merely his mirror image, but his *best* self.

The result: I've yet to meet the person who doesn't think highly of those who think highly of him.

Agreement

I once accompanied a writer friend to a planning committee meeting in order to discover how writers interact with each other. My friend warned me that most writers, like other artists, are loners, highly opinionated, sensitive, and temperamental. A few, he said, are also unduly egocentric. All these personality types would be at the meeting, where unity would be required to shape the direction of the organization. My friend expected chaos.

Instead, under his guiding touch as chairman, I saw the most masterful display of diplomacy in my life. (Diplomacy, according to my friend, is "the art of letting other people have your own way.")

He went to the meeting with clear-cut ideas about the direction the organization should take. Yet he proposed not a single motion. He called on people from the floor to present their points of view, agreeing with at least some part of every comment. Where he disagreed, he would say, "Now who has another opinion on that?" Every statement he made was designed first to *agree* with the speaker, even if the most he could offer in light of his own plans was "Well now, there's a point of view we hadn't considered. Good you raised that thought."

After two hours he rose and said, "Well, this has been incredible. There's not a person in this room that can't take part of the credit for what we've accomplished today." He then proceeded to outline on the blackboard the decisions his colleagues had reached—precisely the plans he brought to the meeting!

My writer friend followed the advice of an old song: "Accentuate the positive, eliminate the negative, and don't mess with Mr. In-Between." I'd change only one word in that lyric: rather than *eliminate* the negative, I'd advise that you *defuse* it.

I knew a real estate broker once who used that technique with great success. Whenever he showed a property to a potential buyer, the prospect would invariably find a defect.

"But the sink is so *old.*"

"Yup," the broker would respond, "if I bought the house I'd replace it, maybe even put in new cabinets. Be at least a thousand bucks. Then you'd have one sharp kitchen."

It was the same with every defect the prospect saw—the broker would agree entirely, even point out problems the buyer hadn't found. The effect was twofold. When the broker stressed the property's *good* points, the buyer believed him. And when he said, "It's still an excellent buy for the price," the prospect usually bought.

When you can agree with a negative comment, you can utterly defuse it. Consider the boss who, after firing off a series of insults, concluded:

"And besides that, you're wearing the ugliest tie I ever saw!"

The employee, after examining the tie carefully, responded, "You're right—it *is* ugly."

What could the boss do but laugh with him and realize that the two of them were in step together after all?

One final word about making illusions work. In that hour of preparation before every concert, I bring myself to a point where it doesn't for one moment enter my mind that anything can go wrong to destroy what I'm achieving in my presentation. I go in so positive that I believe no matter what happens I can harness some reaction from the people I'm working with. I never think of the negative factors.

It is not only your audience that must believe in what you're doing. You must believe, too. That's why these experiments in illusion, so simple and shallow on the surface, are the very best ones to teach you confidence and skill. I promise you'll be performing effects of quite dramatic proportions before you've finished reading this book. But if you're to learn real confidence and skill, you must master these techniques first.

FOUR

You're Stronger Than You Think

People do not lack strength; they lack will.
—VICTOR HUGO

All of us have read newspaper accounts—several of them, no doubt—of ordinary persons who exhibit phenomenal strength in emergencies. The most recent story I recall involved a woman in her fifties who heard moans in her driveway, ran to investigate, and found her son pinned under his car. He'd been working on the exhaust system when the jack slipped.

Without giving it a thought, the woman grabbed the bumper and lifted the vehicle, raising the tire from her son's legs long enough for him to crawl away.

Amazing—yet literally thousands of similar feats have been verified: fragile wives have carried heavy, unconscious husbands from burning homes, or from bathtubs after the men suffered heart attacks. Ordinary men in ordinary physical condition have run great distances to prevent disaster or seek help in emergencies. Such stories of "supernatural" strength appear regularly in the papers.

Danger and emergency aren't the only source of unusual strength, either. A young man I know, of medium build and rather thin, recently moved with his young bride to a third-floor apartment. One of their wedding gifts was a huge refrigerator. Although he and his two burly helpers had no difficulty getting most of their scant belongings into the apartment, the refrigerator proved an insurmountable problem. The steps were narrow, the refrigerator was heavy, and there was simply no way to get a good grip on the sleek surface.

After forty-five minutes of frustration, my young friend simply lost his temper. He threw a strap around the refrigerator, gripped an end in each hand, bent over in front of it and ordered, "Now get it up on my back and keep it balanced!" Without giving it a thought, he carried that refrigerator up two flights of stairs, and the only side effect was sore leg muscles the next day.

Notice that I've used the expression *without giving it a thought* twice. So many aspects of our lives are limited by our own meager expectations. We meekly pigeonhole ourselves, assume that what we are is all we can be. We call it coming to grips with reality, thinking maturely—and certainly there are those who, to paraphrase Saint Paul, "think of themselves more highly than they ought to think." I don't doubt that an unrealistically inflated self-image can lead to misery and failure, but in my experience it's far more common to find people expecting *too little* of themselves. Most of us do that because we've let other people tell us what we *can* and *can't* accomplish.

For example: Until 1954 it was a universally accepted "fact" in track athletics that no human could break the four-minute mile. But Roger Bannister refused to buy that, and that year he ran the mile in 3 minutes, 59.4 seconds.

Bannister's record has been broken many times since then, and today it's almost routine for top athletes to run the mile in under four minutes. But it was Bannister who proved that our limits were not in strength but in will.

You're going to discover some fascinating things about strength in this chapter, and I hope you'll keep in mind that the principles that apply to these simple and entertaining mind games have important implications in everyday life. A few of the effects you'll learn are mere illusion on the same order as those we learned in the previous chapter. Most, although not so dramatic as those mentioned earlier, are examples of strength you didn't know you had.

The following three effects rely not on strength but on the illusion of it. Yet the illusion of strength can be a very useful and pragmatic thing.

Centuries ago Robert Houdin, the great French magician, was approached by the French government to settle a disturbance in a tribe under French control in a distant province. The tribe would submit only to a show of strength, and the French chose to use Houdin rather than the army to make the point. Houdin's performance before the natives was basically magic. The concluding effect involved a small chest that had rested upon the stage all evening. Houdin first called to the stage several of the tribe's strongest young men. Then he gestured toward the chest and asked each of the men to try to pick it up by the handle. They were incapable of budging it, try as they would.

Then Houdin himself lifted the chest with one hand.

Again he challenged the natives, and again they failed.

I don't usually divulge the secrets of conjuring or stage illusions, for I consider such activities unethical, but in this particular case Robert Houdin was simply using an emerging science that was then only in the exploratory stages—electromagnetism. Under the stage was an electromagnet that when turned on forced the chest to adhere to the floor but when shut off made the chest very easy to lift. The illusion worked. In the minds of the natives Robert Houdin was the great white magician who reflected the greater power of the French government.

In recent years on my own TV show and on the Mike Douglas show, I duplicated the test using a small chair. While strong adults could not move it, a small child lifted it over his head with one hand.

I also added a twist. At my command, two or three volunteers held the chair over their heads until I gestured at the chair, "forcing" it to become so heavy that it fell finally to the floor, drawing the volunteers down with it. Yet *I never used electromagnetism.* I used the power of suggestion, planted the idea of the chair's increasing weight so convincingly in the minds of the subjects that they could not continue holding it.

An important point here, to which I'll return later: just as it's possible to persuade others of the illusion of our strength, *we* can be persuaded of false notions of our own weakness.

THE WITHERING TOUCH

Choose as your subject the biggest, strongest man in the room and tell him to put his hands beneath your arms and lift you from the floor. (If you're a rather heavy person yourself and can't find one man who can lift you, perform this effect with two people, one at each side—you'll have to rehearse a few times first.)

After you've been easily lifted, say:

"As every prizefighter knows, there's a nerve center near the chin which, when struck, can render us paralyzed or unconscious. When I find that spot and press it, you will become weak and be unable to lift me."

With your fingertips, studiously explore the man's jaw for the "sensitive" spot. When you find it, you might add effect by marking the spot, at the lower edge of his chin, with a felt-tip pen. Gather your fingers at that point and apply firm, steady pressure. Say:

"Now, try to lift me. You won't be able to."

The subject will find that his strength isn't equal to the task.

The harder he tries, the more difficult it becomes to raise your feet from the floor. Only when you stop pressing will his strength return.

The frailest woman can accomplish as much, not because she's paralyzing the man but because she's forcing him off balance. When the man lifted you the first time, he was using muscles in his shoulders, chest, upper arms, and forearms, but by pushing against his chin and forcing his head back you're making it impossible for him to use those strong muscles without losing his balance. Instead he must rely only on the strength in his forearms, and that's insufficient to lift you.

What's more, the harder he lifts, the more pressure he forces you to apply against his chin, and that pushes him even further off balance.

FINGER POWER

Balance is the key to this effect, too. Have your skeptical friend seat himself in a chair, fold his arms, stretch his legs, and lean well back. Say:

"First, you must relax. Lean back and make yourself comfortable, keeping your arms folded. Now drop your head back and look up at the ceiling."

With your fingertips, search his forehead for a "paralytic zone"; find it and press your forefinger firmly against the spot. After a pause in which you evidence deep concentration, command:

"Now try to rise. Keep your arms folded and get up from the chair. You can't! Harder . . . harder . . . you can't rise!"

And indeed he can't, as your finger continues to press firmly against his forehead. After eight or ten seconds say:

"Now, relax again. Let all tension drain from your body."

Remove your finger from his forehead and tell him:

"Your strength has returned. With your arms still folded, rise from the chair."

He does, with no difficulty. And if you adequately planted

the suggestion that it was the contact with his "paralytic zone" that rendered him helpless, he'll never suspect what really happened—which was simply that you kept him off balance.

If you're sitting in a chair right now, begin to rise. Your very first motion is to move your head and shoulders forward to bring your center of gravity over your legs. All the muscle strength in the world won't get you out of that chair unless you get your head moving first. The stronger your legs push against the floor, the more forcefully you'll thrust yourself right back into the chair. And moving your head forward depends almost entirely on the neck muscles—no match for the strength of a single finger against the forehead.

Requiring your subject to keep his arms folded makes life a bit easier for you since it prevents him from shifting his arm weight forward. Yet unless there are arms on the chair that he can grasp, you'll probably be able to keep him seated even if he has free use of his arms.

PUSH IT DOWN

Perhaps I've never heard people laugh more heartily, actually to tears, than when watching four strong men struggle against my one hand in this supposed contest of strength. I promise you it'll be the memorable highlight of any party. This is how it went the last time I performed it at an informal party attended by several celebrities in a Manhattan penthouse:

At my request, the hostess brought a broom into the living room. I selected two volunteers, had them stand side by side and each grasp the broom handle palms up. Dropping a piece of paper on the floor, I asked them to touch the handle end of the broom to the paper while the other end pointed to the ceiling. They did so without effort.

"With one hand I can keep you from doing it again," I challenged. They responded with guffaws. I confess my heart always warms in anticipation at that point.

I instructed the men to hold the pole parallel with the floor again and placed two fingers just inside the hand closest to the end intended to touch the paper.

"When you're ready, gentlemen," I announced.

The men thrust furiously in what they thought was a downward motion, but instead we proceeded to move about four feet across the room.

The hostess brought us a longer pole, and now two additional men took part, each grasping the pole in open hands, palms upward. Again I laid my open hand just inside the hand closest to the tip. Again the men thrust, and again the pole traveled forward instead of downward. Each man dropped lower. Finally we were on our knees, two feet from the floor and two yards beyond the paper, each of us struggling and all the guests laughing until their sides ached.

Here's the secret: Instead of pressing upward as the audience and the challengers assumed I was doing, I actually forced the bar forward, parallel to the floor. In that way the strength of the challengers was converted from downward to forward motion, and since that moved the pole away from the target, they actually had to combat their own forward efforts with backward efforts to keep the pole over the paper. After a few practice attempts to position your hand properly, you'll have great fun with this effect.

We all have physical strength of which we're not aware, as I've said, and the following four effects are based on that. Let me emphasize the need for concentration, however. As I said in chapter 2, virtually all successful effects require *ability to concentrate,* and for those whose self-image is one of weakness, that self-image acts as an autosuggestion to produce weakness even when it doesn't physically exist. Anyone who is physically normal can produce the following effects, but you must concentrate on that knowledge and assurance, *envisioning the act completed* (as outlined in chapter 2) and *eliminating all doubt.*

LIFT THE HANDS

While standing, shape your hand like a claw, press the fingers against the top of your head and challenge anyone to break the "magnetic contact" that now keeps your fingers attached to your skull. Explain that jerking and bending back individual fingers is not permitted.

Someone is likely to comment that, with you in a standing position, he can't get the leverage needed to exert strong upward pressure. He has a good point. Agree with him and say: "To give you some help, I'll sit in this chair and place my hand flat on my head." Do so, instructing the challenger to try again. If he pulls your wrist sideways, pitting his arm strength against your weight, allow your head and entire body to follow your hand in that direction. Explain that he must pull your arm straight upward—otherwise he will succeed only in pulling you off the chair.

As long as you concentrate on keeping your hand in contact with your head, he'll fail to overcome the "magnetic force."

Now you're ready to make the ultimate challenge. Say:

"This fellow needs some help. May I have another volunteer?"

While you remain seated, position a volunteer at each side. Lock your fingers together and place your folded hands palms down against the top of your head. Challenge each man to lift the hand closest to him.

If the men are strong, chances are they'll actually lift you from the chair—but they *won't* separate your hands from your head.

There's no trick at all involved. The easiest way to do it is to keep your elbows down and forward, but a person of average strength can get the same result no matter what position his arm is in. The muscles involved are sufficiently strong to hold the weight of your entire body, and when a challenger tries to separate your hand from your head, the most that he can accomplish is to lift all of you.

FIST ON FIST

Although it won't be apparent to most of your audience, this effect simply illustrates that a strong push—using your large chest muscles—is more effective than a hard pull relying basically on a challenger's arm strength.

Extend your arms straight forward, close your fists, and plant one on top of the other. Say to the challenger:

"My fists are now sealed together. Stand directly in front of me and grasp one fist in each hand. Now, while I press them up and down, you try to pull them left and right. Your pressure must be steady—no jerking."

No one will be able to dislodge your fists—and if you plant the suggestion properly, no one will duplicate your success either. You've led your audience to believe that the key is in pressing the fists together vertically—up and down. In fact, the major effort is in pushing them together horizontally, as though the knuckles were touching instead of fist-on-fist. As others try, simply emphasize the need for strenuous up and down pressure. Then casually separate their fists.

What if someone catches on to the technique? Be alert to that possibility. As soon as you find significant resistance to your efforts stop and say:

"That's too easy. I like a real challenge. What if I separate your fists using just two fingers?"

When the mocking laughter dies down, close your own fists and point the forefinger straight at your challenger. Say:

"Like this!"

Sweeping your hands in opposite directions, clip the challenger's fists briskly, forcing them apart. The key, although no one will realize it, is that you broke your own rule against jerking by riveting the audience's attention on the impossible task you've set for your fingers.

On occasion, a spoilsport will insist that *he* can separate *your* fists with *his* fingers, too. That's a challenge you can't laugh off, nor can you permit yourself to be defeated, even if you must stoop to trickery—and you must.

Position your fists one above the other as before and invite the challenger to whack as hard and as long as he likes. He'll collapse from exhaustion or embarrassment long before your fists separate.

The reason is that this time you've secretly extended the thumb of your lower hand upward into the grip of your upper fist. Now the two hands are *truly* sealed.

FOUR-MAN FINGER LIFT

Famous magicians have been performing this feat on stage for many years, persuading audience and participants it was accomplished through a mystic power imbued in the four lifters by the magician himself. In fact, it's simply another example of the unrealized strength in all of us.

Choose a man or woman weighing no more than 130 pounds and four men of average strength. Tell the audience:

"Any one of these men could lift this woman, and if they all tried at once it would be no challenge. But what if each of them used only *one* finger? Could they do it?"

Doubt will reign. Yet the lift is easily made. Position the strongest man behind the woman, an index finger under each of her arms. Two more volunteers kneel next to each foot and place a finger beneath it. The final man stands in front of the woman and holds a finger sideways beneath her chin.

Count to three and command them to lift. The woman will rise at least a foot from the floor.

THE RIGID BODY

I'm not discussing this effect in order that you may perform it. In fact, you should *not.* Several people have been seriously injured by it, even when it was attempted by skilled performers. I explain it here only because it illustrates so well the hidden strength many of us possess.

A few years ago, I performed this effect on Johnny Carson's show—and Johnny Carson himself was the Rigid Body. Before the show aired, I insisted on seeing Carson backstage so that we could rehearse. Anyone who has been a guest on "The Tonight Show" knows that it is rarely permitted that a guest see Carson before airtime, but I had to be certain that he could handle the stress. I repeat, it's a potentially dangerous test.

I had other guests lift Johnny off his feet and hold him in a horizontal position while I slipped one straight chair beneath his heels and another beneath his head, neck, and shoulders. Not only did he remain rigid in that position, but actually supported the weight of another guest, who stood with one foot on his chest and another on his lower abdomen.

Since then I've performed the same test with Eddie Albert and Mike Douglas and on Bill Boggs's New York television show. There's no trick involved. The weight is borne by the very strong muscles of our shoulders, buttocks, back, and legs. If the muscles or skeleton are abnormally weak, however, very serious injuries can occur.

THE RIGID ARM

With this effect and the following one, we're looking ahead to the next chapter on suggestion. Not that strength isn't important here—it is. But unlike the muscles in the previous effects, the ones you'll use now might feel particularly stressed, suggesting to you that they'll fail. You must counter that thought with a positive autosuggestion of success.

Ask a volunteer to stand beside you, the two of you facing in the same direction. Take a short step forward and extend the arm nearest the volunteer straight out in front of him so that it's level with your shoulder. Say:

"Place your one hand, palm downward, just below my shoulder and your other, palm upward, on my lower arm. Now pump my arm up and down as though it were a pump handle."

Allow your arm to move easily. When the volunteer has rehearsed the movements sufficiently, tell him:

"Now, through sheer willpower, I'm going to freeze my arm, forcing it to become rigid. Please attempt to pump it again. Begin lightly, then hard . . . harder . . ." After a few seconds, when it becomes obvious to all that your arm cannot be moved, say, "That's enough."

Several physical factors have contributed to your success. The strength in the volunteer's lower arm is inhibited by his upwardly twisted wrist, and his upper hand is at a point in the fulcrum of your arm and shoulder where its effect is drastically reduced. What's more, since you're a step in front of him, he's somewhat off balance. Yet if you use another subject in place of yourself, you'll find that most people can't prevent the arm from being pumped, strain though they will.

The key is that *you must actually create and accept the image of your arm utterly riveted in place.* Envision a steel I-beam —continuous, solid, inflexible—bent at a right angle to form your outstretched arm, shoulder, and side. It is no more capable of bending than if your whole being were formed of a single block of granite.

In order to prevent excessive strain on the muscles, continue this effect only long enough to make the point.

Here's a bonus to the RIGID ARM: you can pass your power on to another volunteer. Have the subject take your place, extending his strong arm (usually left for lefthanded people, right for righthanded) in front of the person doing the pumping. Then say:

"Your arm is becoming rigid. Close your eyes and imagine your arm extended. It is not flesh and bone but steel, a steel girder, bent at your shoulder and continuing along your side into your legs, then anchored in the floor. Can you *see* it in your mind? Can you *feel* its solidness in your body, in your shoulder, in the length of your arm? Your arm is inflexible steel, many times stronger than the strongest man. You can *feel* the firmness of it, *see* it in your mind."

Instruct the pumper to begin with minimal pressure and

gradually increase it while you continue to comment, "strong, firm, hard as steel."

When it's obvious that the arm won't bend, end the experiment.

The RIGID ARM is one of my favorite tests, for it goes beyond entertainment to illustrate the extent to which our own beliefs limit or release our capabilities. Most people "know" they *can't* hold their arm out at an awkward angle and resist the two-handed strength of another. Because we "know" it, we psychologically surrender before putting up a fight—and of course we're defeated.

Sadly, many people go through life declaring their defeat, and there are always those who'll be glad to encourage the losers—telling them what they can't do in order to make themselves appear superior or in control.

I was performing in California recently when I developed stiffness in my neck and shoulders. I decided to get a quick massage, and since I was in a hurry to catch a plane (as usual), I went to the nearest facility—which happened to be a holistic health establishment. The practitioner, before getting to work on my stiff muscles, asked me to stand tall, stare straight ahead, and extend my left arm forward.

Somewhat puzzled, I obeyed. He grasped my wrist, his palm downward, instructing me to resist the pressure, which I did.

"Now, keeping your head straight forward, turn your eyes to the extreme left," he told me. "I want you to resist the pressure again." This time the arm yielded to his strength.

"Just as I suspected," he told me. "You have some serious blockages in the electrical, magnetic, and gravitational flow through your body. Some major tsubos in the prime meridians are all screwed up. It'll take us at least half a dozen sessions to get you balanced."

Now I understood. He was using a natural psychological phenomenon to persuade me that I was weaker than I really was. It was an unconscionable dishonesty—by having me look to the left, the huckster had broken the concentration required to keep my arm rigid.

I told him to repeat the diagnosis, and of course it was a simple thing, now that I knew what he intended to do, to envision the arm of invisible steel. He grew frustrated and puzzled.

"Use *both* your hands," I virtually ordered. Again he had no success. I turned and left the office—and never did get a massage.

In a recent study college students, while listening to irritating and noisy music, were asked to extend an arm forward and resist efforts by experimenters to press it downward. The young people failed the challenge.

In the second half of the test the students listened to peaceful, relaxing music. Again they were asked to extend their arms, and this time they were able to resist the pressure.

I've no doubt this effect can be offset by suggestion, even autosuggestion. Some youngsters are able to study more effectively while listening to acid rock than when no music at all is playing, and others work harder *with* that noise than *without* it. My point is this: when your attention is distracted from confidence in your ability, your strength wanes.

To reach your highest potential, whether physical or mental, you must actively concentrate on the strength you know you have.

The huckster distracted my attention by having me glance to the side, and because I did not know his intention, I allowed him to do it.

How much of your potential for achievement is destroyed because (1) you have a self-image of weakness and defeatism, or (2) someone or something sidetracks your concentration on the strengths you know you have?

Have Confidence in Your Strength

Robert Bahr, a professional writer for twenty years and a friend of mine, has lectured to many of his colleagues on writer's block, a condition in which the writer simply stares at a blank page, unable to write. Bahr is an authority on the subject by virtue of the fact that he has not once suffered from the problem.

"Writer's block is nothing but a lack of self-confidence," he says. "Perhaps the writer's mind is a little foggy that morning, or he has a cold and doesn't feel up to writing. So he accepts an autosuggestion: 'I don't *feel* up to writing,' becomes 'I *can't* write—the words won't come.' "

Bahr tells other writers to override the negative suggestion by implanting a positive one. "Read the best stuff you've written so that you *know* how good you are. Write fun letters to friends, make an entry in your journal. Then sit down and get to work. It might not be your best at first (who was it that said, 'There's no such thing as good writing, only good rewriting'), but once you get involved, the work will improve."

In the business world many capable people fail to be promoted simply because they lack confidence. They have the ability to do more complex and rewarding jobs, but by their attitudes they say, "I'm afraid I'll fail." Their lack of confidence is evidenced in their limp handshakes, their unwillingness to confront superiors with a friendly yet steady, unfaltering gaze. Their whole demeanor suggests lack of self-assurance. We all instinctively read such signs in each other, and no boss can be blamed for concluding that such an individual isn't quite right for the job—the person himself is saying as much.

Be Committed to Concentration

Some years ago two actresses, both veterans and consummate performers, were in the same Broadway play together. As might be expected, competitive tensions ran high, each competing for the limelight, each attempting to upstage the other and reaching into their large bags of dirty tricks to break the other's concentration.

As the story goes, one night actress A planned the stroke that would finally devastate actress B. She persuaded the prop man to ring the telephone during her competitor's monologue, shattering the mood and leaving the actress at a loss as to how to respond to the ringing phone.

It went almost according to plan. Alone on the stage, actress B was swept up in some important lines when the telephone rang. As the prankster came on stage beaming, the other woman, maintaining her composure, answered the phone. The veteran actresses' eyes met.

"It's for you, darling," announced actress B, laying the receiver on the table and walking off stage.

Another actress, Katharine Hepburn, perhaps the greatest of all time, simply won't tolerate any challenges to her ability to concentrate. Recently she literally stopped a play, turned to the audience and berated a woman for taking flashbulb pictures during the show. The woman left in tears. On another occasion she scolded a man for resting his feet on the stage. She said that it not only changed the set as the audience viewed it but affected her whole perception and concentration.

One of the most common ways that people allow their concentration to be distracted is by assuming too many responsibilities. As one executive in a hotel chain where I was performing told me recently, "I was doing a few jobs very well, really concentrating on them, and my boss got jealous. He thought I was after his job. So he gave me twice the workload—and now I've more than I can handle."

The circumstances of our lives often fracture our ability to concentrate on our strengths. Bills, children, marital discord, illness, a multitude of diverse responsibilities all shatter the single-mindedness needed if we are to develop our strengths to their maximum. Although Thoreau explained it differently, I think that's what he had in mind when he summarized his approach to life with the single word "Simplify!" I can offer no better advice.

FIVE

Just a Suggestion

Belief is the natural possession of beings possessing minds.
—MARTIN D'ARCY, The Nature of Belief

Not long ago I read of a medical study in which placebos—sugar pills containing no medication—were found twice as effective in curing headaches and minor aches and pains as were real drugs. Of course there was nothing in the sugar pill that would cure any symptoms, yet placebos are frequently prescribed by doctors when an ailment is diagnosed as psychosomatic—resulting not from a physical problem but a state of mind. Some people convince themselves that they are ill, and that autosuggestion is sufficient to produce genuine and often agonizing pain, physical crippling, and, in rare cases, death. (It is that very principle that can make the curse of a witch doctor fatal to those who believe in it.)

As the placebo study illustrates, illness caused by suggestion can also be cured by suggestion. That's why the placebo often can be potent therapy indeed. Mothers often use it without a thought when their child rushes into the house wailing and clutching a skinned knee. A bit of salve, a bandage, a kiss from Mom, and the suggestion "It's all better" make the tears magically disappear.

Let me show you right now how you can make suggestion work for you in a simple experiment. I call it the HAND WARMING TEST, and it has been used by physicians and psychologists in recent years to reduce or eliminate the pain of migraine headaches, possibly by reducing blood flow to the brain. Obviously you will not try this test when your hands are already warm from washing or hard work; they must feel the same temperature as the rest of your body.

Sit in a chair, and if you want proof that the test works, hold a sensitive thermometer in your hand for a few minutes. Then take a reading. Now imagine that both of your hands are submerged in hot water. When I say "imagine," I mean *remember*. Did you wash dishes last night? Did you draw a bath? Do you remember the feeling of the hot water on your hands? It is this vivid recall that makes suggestion most effective. You are not *pretending* now that your hands are in hot water; you are actually *reliving* the experience. Feel the needlelike pangs of the hot water against your skin. Visualize the wrinkling of your fingertips. Is the water too hot to endure? No, you can stand it—but it certainly is *hot*.

You will soon notice that one hand feels warmer than the other. Shift the thermometer to the warmer hand and concentrate all your attention on it.

Now you *know* that your hand is getting warmer. You can feel it. Tell yourself what you know: "My hand is getting warmer." Repeat it silently or aloud. Continue the test for at least five minutes so that the thermometer will have the time to register the change.

Although the temperature will increase by between one-half degree and three degrees, your thermometer might not be sensitive enough to detect it. Whether it does or not, you certainly will have felt the difference.

If you are a football or hockey fan, you know that hardly a

season goes by without some outstanding player having a violent collision yet continuing through the game with no indication of injury. Only when the game is over and he enters the dressing room does he become aware of the serious pain he is suffering. The athlete had been so eager to play and win that he gave himself an unconscious suggestion: "I feel no pain and am not injured."

It's this capacity to accept self-generated suggestion (autosuggestion) that separates outstanding athletes who can endure the pain of overwhelming effort from those with equal physical capacity who accomplish far less.

Don't confuse suggestion and autosuggestion with the mythical "hypnotic trance." In spite of the soothing talk, penetrating stares, and swinging chains employed by sideshow magicians, there is no such thing as a hypnotic trance. I still have a standing offer to pay twenty thousand dollars to anyone who can prove otherwise. I do not expect ever to lose this money, since laboratory tests have shown that when supposedly under hypnosis, subjects have precisely the same physiological responses as they normally do. Even their electroencephalogram readings are the same—they are certainly not asleep in any sense. They are fully alert and know exactly what's going on.

The story was the same a hundred years ago and more when hypnotism was called mesmerism, although the whole procedure was even more flamboyant than it is today. Often wearing a dramatic cape, the mesmerist made long, flowing gestures before his subject, which supposedly lulled the individual into an altered state of consciousness. One rather critical observer of the day dismissed mesmerism as the product of the subject's active imagination. The critic was Benjamin Franklin.

Today if someone were to ask you to lie on a table or sit in a chair while he made exaggerated sweeping gestures over your body, face, arms, and legs, you might be tempted to laugh, but if you were first conditioned to believe that these gestures were sending a mysterious magnetic force or fluid from the mesmerist's hands and eyes to your own body, you might take it quite seriously. And if you were receptive to the mesmerist's suggestion, you might experience the convulsive response that was the hallmark of the state of mesmerism.

Today mesmerism has given way to the fashionable trance through which, according to Hollywood, a villainous hypnotist can cast highly moral people into a zombielike stupor and force them to commit heinous crimes. In fact, many educators, entertainers, and physicians have almost that naive a view of hypnosis.

Sideshow hypnotists sometimes like to induce a state called catalepsy, in which a subject is put into a difficult position and told to hold it longer than the average person would consider possible. The subject also might be told it is impossible for him to move, and he might accept the suggestion. To prove to you that no special trance is required, let me show you how you can use catalepsy yourself in an interesting mind game.

Challenge a group of friends at a party with the announcement: "I'm ten times stronger than you are. I'll bet you couldn't even hold a feather for twenty minutes."

When the challenge is accepted—and it will be—produce enough small chicken feathers to go around and tell each participant to hold one in each hand, arms outstretched in front of him with the palms down, for twenty minutes. Few will be able to do it for even five minutes, not because the feather is heavy but because their arms are. Actually, the muscles involved could do the job easily, but after a few minutes pain develops that few people are trained to ignore.

Of course, in many contexts we do ignore the pain—for example, the athletes I mentioned earlier. Painters, secretaries, mailmen, and many others stress limited muscle groups every day without noticing the pain that might make you and me give up the effort. The difference is that *they are not thinking about the pain but about the work they're doing.* They endure by concentrating on something other than the pain.

That's how you will prove that you're ten times stronger than your friends. After the last one gives up, take a quarter from your pocket and ask everyone to agree that it is ten times heavier than the feather. If they do not, add another quarter to the first to clinch your argument. Have someone you trust take a wristwatch and tell you when to begin. At the command, extend your arm and proceed to concentrate on something other than pain.

Personally, I prefer to concentrate on reading a book. It isn't the easiest trick to turn the pages with one hand, but that too becomes an effective subject of concentration. I admit that I have an unusual ability to concentrate—after all, I've been doing this for most of my life and it is my profession—so I can keep my mind on the book even when friends are heckling and desperately trying to convince me that my arm is growing weary. I have a friend who is unable to concentrate on reading, but because he is a very opinionated fellow, he uses the twenty minutes to give a soapbox lecture on his latest gripe to his now captive audience. He becomes so involved that he grows livid with passion and is thoroughly disappointed when the timer announces that the twenty minutes have passed.

Incidentally, promoters of the Lamaze method of natural childbirth (who, I am delighted to know, have referred to my work in a number of their educational films) recommend concentration on another subject as one method of helping women in labor through childbirth.

The following tests are designed to show you the power of suggestion in action. You and your friends will find what some psychologists and most sensitives have known all along: that we are all far more influenced by suggestion—from authority figures, news media, our upbringing, and our own conditioning —than we would ever suspect.

THE CONFETTI RACE

You'll need two players, two spoons, two paper bags, two bowls of confetti or paper shavings, and two good blindfolds for this test. Seat the players opposite each other at a table and give them a spoon and a bowl of confetti. Show them the paper bags, each with a line drawn two-thirds up from the bottom. Explain that you will blindfold the competitors and that they will be required to fill the bags to the line but not beyond, testing their skills in judging weight. When a player thinks he has reached the line, he is to make the announcement and then wait for the other player to do the same—he is not to remove the blindfold. Whoever is closer to the line at the finish is the winner.

Assure the players that they may lift the bags to weigh them as they go along to help them to guess when they have reached the mark. Emphasize that confetti is very light.

After carefully blindfolding the players (soft balls of cotton over the eyes held in place by a snug handkerchief usually prevents peeking), open the bags. Be sure to signal all observers to keep silent as they discover that the bags have no bottoms.

Start the race and cheer the players on. As surely as the sun will rise in the morning, first one player and then the other will, after much weighing, conclude that he has reached the mark.

With blindfolds removed, the subjects will discover how uncritically they accepted your suggestion that the weight was increasing in the bags.

GLUED EYELIDS

You can perform this test with a small group or a single person. Ask the subject to be seated. Create an atmosphere conducive to concentration. Tell the subjects:

"We are going to try a test of simple concentration. I want you to sit back easily, gaze straight ahead, and close your eyes. All eyes closed. Now imagine that you have a hole in the center of your head. It's rather large—you can see through it to the ceiling. Can you picture it? Keep your eyes closed, and start looking upward. . . . Try to see that imaginary hole. . . . You can't quite see it, because it is too far back, but keep looking farther upward . . . farther upward. . . . You can almost see it now. You know it's there. . . . Keep visualizing it as you look higher . . . higher. . . . Now you see it. Now you're actually looking through it, through the top of your head. . . . Keep looking upward . . . upward. . . ."

By studying the expressions on the subjects' faces, you'll recognize which ones have reached a deep level of concentration and are actually visualizing the hole and perhaps even the ceiling above their heads. You might address individually those subjects who do not seem to be concentrating deeply enough, or you might select the subject who appears most receptive to the suggestion and work directly with him or her. Say:

"While you are looking at the hole, you will not be able to open your eyes. They are glued tightly shut. Try to open your eyes . . . you can't. Keep looking upward . . . to the ceiling. . . . Try to open your eyes. They are glued shut! Tightly shut. . . ."

Continue to repeat your statement in a normal volume but in a commanding, authoritative tone as the subjects try to open their eyes. Then, easing your tone, tell them:

"Now, relax. . . . Forget the image you've created. . . . Just relax. . . . Don't worry about that hole in the top of your head . . . it isn't there. . . . Don't try to look for it, just relax. Now open your eyes."

Most subjects will indeed open their eyes, some blinking and bewildered, convinced that you had some peculiar power over them. In fact, they themselves were responsible for their "glued" eyelids, for they accepted your suggestion that they could visualize a hole in their heads, and by staring upward they made it physically impossible to open their eyes.

To help assure the success of this effect, precede it with your best illusions from chapter 3 in order to gain the confidence of the subjects. Do not try to prolong the effect more than a few seconds—eight or ten at most—or you risk having a subject analyze what is happening, reject the suggestion to continue staring at the hole in his head, and prematurely open his eyes.

CLASPED HANDS

Start by telling each person to clasp his own hands together with thumbs and fingers interlocked. Demonstrate by folding your own hands, and check to see that everyone has followed your instructions exactly.

As you raise your folded hands outward, say:

"Keeping our fingers locked snugly, we're going to raise our arms out in front of us. Keep your arms straight and raise them in front of you, turning palms outward so that you can see the backs of your hands and fingers."

Demonstrate how this should be done with your own interlocked fingers, and check to see that everyone still has his fingers securely interlocked. Say:

"Now, keeping your arms perfectly straight and your fingers interlocked, raise your arms straight upward, over your head. Look at the backs of your fingers. Keep pressing firmly toward the ceiling. . . ."

When all have reached that position and maintained it for a few seconds, you can announce, "Now try to draw your hands apart. You can't separate them. . . . They're locked together! Firmly locked! They won't come apart. . . ."

Keep an eye on each participant, and if one or two seem to be "unlocking," urge them to lift their hands, "higher . . . higher . . . now pull harder!"

Pushing the hands upward forces the fingers together and nullifies all efforts to pull the hands apart. The key is your persuasive insistence that the hands be pushed higher and higher. Only when the subject rejects that suggestion can he succeed in separating his hands.

To conclude the test, say:

"Now, hold it . . . stop trying to pull your hands apart. Bring them straight downward. Keep your arms forward. . . ."

As the participants reach that position, urge them: "Keep

watching your hands as you turn palms toward you. Now draw them apart, slowly. Very slowly apart."

Here, as before, demonstrate the procedure and, by separating your own hands, suggest that everyone's hands are now unlocked. The reason you should demonstrate the unlocking is that some subjects might still find their hands locked simply on the basis of suggestion. Use the opportunity to demonstrate how effectively the test worked. Then emphasize the order: "Slowly . . . slowly . . . relax. . . ." Soothing words and touch will always bring the predicament to an end.

TELL-A-CARD

In chapter 3 I explained that every successful illusion results from a successful suggestion. Now let me go a step further. I believe that most "extrasensory" achievements are related to (although not explained by) suggestion or imagination—suggestion is the gate that opens the subject's mind to the "extrasensory" potential. You will succeed in achieving complex effects to the degree that you master the art of giving authoritative and persuasive suggestions to your subjects.

One of the best tests of your ability to implant a suggestion is the TELL-A-CARD game. It depends entirely on the suggestion, for the secret of the effect is so simple that your subjects, allowed to consider the obvious, will catch on.

Have a subject thoroughly shuffle a deck of cards and spread the deck faceup so that everyone can see that they are well mixed. Gather the cards into a pack and place it face down. Have a subject cut the pack in the middle and place the top half face down a few inches beyond the bottom half. Lift the card from the top of the nearest heap, study it, and say:

"This card will tell me the name of the card on the far heap." Name that card and casually place the card you are holding on the top of the near heap.

Now turn up the card on the far heap. It will be the card you announced. Put it back in the pack, place the near heap on top of the far one, and say:

"Will someone cut the pack and we'll try it again."

Place the top half beyond the other as you did the first time and examine the card on the near heap. Announce the card on the top of the far pile.

You could go on playing this game all night, and some subjects will never catch on as long as you *keep them wondering how the card you examine gives you the clue to the card on the far pack. You must continue to reinforce that suggestion.*

Of course the card you look at doesn't tell you anything about the card on the other heap—it tells you what the next card on that heap will be. At the outset, when you spread the cards faceup to show they are shuffled, note the first card in the pack, the one at the extreme left or right. When the pack is placed face down again and cut into two heaps, place them so that this card becomes the top one of the far heap. Now you know the card you are going to identify, but you must still study the card on the top of the near heap for two reasons: to suggest that the game is far more complex than it really is; to give you the opportunity to memorize the card on the top of the near heap.

When you put the near heap on top of the far one, the card you have examined will be on top. No matter where the deck is cut, you can still make sure that card is on top of the far heap.

As I've said, some people will not catch on even if you continue this game all night, but others are not so suggestible, so I don't recommend repeating it more than half a dozen times. A good way to "cap the climax" is to announce before the last play, "I'm going to try to concentrate very hard this time, and perhaps I can name both of these cards—the top one on each heap—without looking at either of them." Place the fingers of both hands on the near heap and appear deeply thoughtful. Say:

"We have here—" and name the card that you know is on the far heap. Lift the card off the top of the near heap and glance at it. Of course it won't be the card you named. Then say:

"And the card on the far heap is—" Name the card in your

hand. Lift the card from the far heap, allowing no one to see it. Examine it, smile, and throw both cards faceup on the table.

FIRE AND ICE

It has been reported that some people are so susceptible to suggestion that, blindfolded and told that they will be touched with a white hot poker, they immediately develop a large blister when their arms are touched—with an ice cube. An experiment based on the same principle but less violent is FIRE AND ICE.

Tell your subject that you are going to blow out a match and then touch his hand immediately with the tip. Assure him that you have done this before and he won't be seriously burned, but you wish to test his reflexes. Ask him to tell you when the pain becomes too great to endure. Explain that he must put his hands behind his back so that he cannot respond even before he has been touched.

Light the match so that he can hear it and smell the sulfur. Blow it out and immediately touch his hand with the edge of an ice cube. Chances are he'll tell you instantly that it's too hot.

Let me tell you of a game a psychology instructor and I once played—one that I do not recommend unless it's germane to the lesson, since some people are particularly open to suggestion and can become physically ill because of it.

When the class began, the instructor had on his desk a jar half full of clear liquid with the word "chloroform" printed on the label. He began by removing the lid and asking every student to check his watch because during the class they would be conducting a research project to determine how much chloroform will evaporate in thirty minutes. At the back of the jar, about a quarter of an inch above the liquid, the instructor applied a piece of tape. He then took an informal poll of how much chloroform the students thought would evaporate, confirming the suggestion that a certain amount—perhaps half or three-quarters—would do so. Before starting the day's instruction he also pointed out that anyone feeling slightly uncomfortable about the aroma should let him know.

Ten minutes later the instructor wrinkled his nose, indicating that the evaporating chloroform bothered him. He tilted the jar slightly to show that the liquid was already below the line of tape he had applied to the back of the jar. The angle at which he held the jar increased the effect.

After about fifteen minutes the instructor asked, "Are any of you becoming as bothered by the smell as I am?" Several students nodded, their faces reflecting minor nausea.

At that moment I rose from my chair, walked to the front of the room, and took a good swallow from the jar—it contained only water.

Do these experiments show you how easily we are disposed to accept inaccurate and even negative suggestions? But here is the wonderful thing about suggestion: just as we can use it to create an unpleasant "aroma," we can produce pleasant and cheering effects as well.

Suggestion is at the core of every successful program in motivation and all effective guides to positive thinking.

Here are some ways you can use suggestion to improve and perhaps even change your life.

ALTERING MOODS

Some time ago, during one of my many appearances on the Mike Douglas show, a well-known Broadway and film actress volunteered to be my subject. We did a test that I call "Obsession," in which the subject is made to respond exactly the same way no matter how many times she is given a choice and no matter how many alternatives are available. I remember the show well because the actress was absolutely baffled over her inability to respond in any but the predetermined fashion.

I'll now produce the same effect with you. You can participate as you read along.

Pick up a pencil and sit at a table. Every time you see the

two words "Tap, tap," tap the pencil on the table twice. Let's practice. "Tap, tap." (You should have tapped the pencil twice.)

"Now, I want you to think about SUNSHINE. You can either think of the word as it appears on the page, or better yet, envision a cloudless summer sky filled with brilliant SUN-SHINE. Feel the heat of it, the glory of dazzling SUNSHINE. Every time you tap the pencil, envision as intensely as you can SUNSHINE.

"Tap, tap," SUNSHINE.

"Tap, tap," SUNSHINE.

As you read the next few sentences, every time you see "Tap, tap," think SUNSHINE. (Did you just do it?) Each time as I continue to write the words "Tap, tap," you should tap the pencil again and think SUNSHINE. "Tap, tap." Did you do it? If you have not done it every time you saw "Tap, tap," then you should go back to the beginning and start again.

"Tap, tap."

You might see the "Tap, tap" in the middle of the sentence, or perhaps you see "Tap, tap" later. Each time associate "Tap, tap" with SUNSHINE.

Now I'm going to ask you to try *not* to think of SUNSHINE when you tap the pencil to the table. But the fact is that you will not be able to keep SUNSHINE out of your mind when you hear the pencil tap. As soon as you "Tap, tap" now, you will think, SUNSHINE. I no longer need suggest SUNSHINE for you have conditioned *yourself* to think of it. "Tap, tap." Notice how SUNSHINE pops into your mind? Try not to think of it, just "Tap, tap." You thought of SUNSHINE again! Try it again by yourself. You see!

Here's how to make use of the "Tap, tap" suggestion. (Did you envision SUNSHINE?) When the weather is unpleasant or you're in a sour mood, simply tap your pencil on the table twice. You'll immediately envision SUNSHINE. Relax, enjoy it, and let your mood elevate. (It's certainly less expensive than flying to the Bahamas!)

Although you might not recognize the fact, you already respond to specific suggestions by developing various moods. Some thoughts invariably depress you. So do some people and places. If you can't avoid them, why not give yourself a countersuggestion response by thinking of something pleasant whenever you encounter them?

Certain music, perhaps poetry, people, and places, always set you in a positive mood. Try to be conscious of the uplifting factors in your life, and when your spirits need boosting, utilize them.

PREPARING FOR TOMORROW

In studying the lives of many outstanding men and women I have found at least one common characteristic: each person appears to have practiced autosuggestion, although most probably didn't realize it. If you are the sort of person who can lose yourself in a good book or movie, not only sympathize with others but almost feel that you're in their shoes, if you're moved by an idea, a song, a game, or a poem to the point that you forget where you are, then I have no doubt that you too can use autosuggestion to obtain remarkable results.

Whether you intend to be a professional athlete, a performer, a successful businessman, or whatever, your ultimate success is merely the top rung of a long, long ladder, and the advice I'm going to give you must be applied on every single rung.

There are many ways to use autosuggestion to increase your chances for achievement, but the one I have found most common to successful people is the suggestion that leads to *pre-experience*. As I mentioned earlier, you can virtually live through a situation before it takes place, whether it's a ball game, a dance, an interview, or an examination, to learn what to expect and to prepare for it.

Pre-experiencing a situation is not the same as daydreaming. Daydreams are fantasies, wishful thinking; a pre-experience is the detailed pre-creation of an occurrence, both positive and negative aspects, with no "editing" or wish projection on your part.

Begin by relaxing your body and mind as outlined in chapter 2.

Next recognize the surroundings of your pre-experience in detail. Study the other people involved—they can't see you now, so you can stare at them as long as you wish. Do their faces tell you of their strengths and weaknesses? What about their posture? Do you suppose, now that you're sizing them up, that one approach might be more effective than another?

Try to make this moment come alive for you so that it actually takes place. Now let the scene unfold in the present tense. Let it really happen precisely as it is going to happen.

Suppose you are pre-experiencing an exam. If you are deeply enough involved, you will recognize that the questions follow a pattern similar to those on the instructor's previous tests. You will see that there are whole blocks of questions on material that the instructor has emphasized in lectures. You might find yourself saying, "I should have known he would ask that essay question—it's a natural."

I had a student actually come up to me after a performance in Las Vegas a couple of years ago to tell me that he believed he owed his graduation to the fact that he had pre-experienced some crucial questions on his final exam.

Perhaps you have a leading role in a play. By pre-experiencing the entire performance you will recognize how effectively a gesture or movement can dress up otherwise drab dialogue. You can prepare yourself for someone else's missed cue or outright flub and watch yourself weave your "save" into the script. You can make suggestions to the director, for you've already seen your ideas played successfully through pre-experience.

The athlete who can watch himself from the sidelines while he plays the game has an enormous advantage. Notice the first indication that the pitch will be low and inside. Feel your body adjusting naturally to a curve that will cross the plate; in the field, note how you adapt your motion naturally to get to where that high fly ball is.

Visualization, as I described in chapter 2, is of utmost importance in helping you to achieve all of your potential strength. For many years Russian athletes have been trained in the use of visualization. A Western hockey player at the Olympics has reported walking into the Russian team's dressing room to discover those players in deep concentration, their legs moving along the floor as they sat on the benches, their eyes closed, while they *pre-experienced* the game that would soon take place. This kind of rehearsal links in a spontaneous way the ideal and the real.

Jean-Claude Killy, the skier, was unable to prepare for an important event because of injury, so while he lay in bed immobile, he rehearsed his performance mentally. Killy left his sickbed with impossibly little time to prepare for competition. Yet he entered the contest and won, later commenting that he had been practicing in his mind all along.

The great Russian weightlifter Vasily Alekseyev spends a great deal of time standing and staring down at the weights before gripping them. I often wondered what was going through his mind, and recently he answered the question for reporters. He said, in effect, "I never attempt to lift up the weight until I first watch myself taking it in my hands, lifting it, and pressing it over my head."

In the same way, detail by detail, you can pre-experience the questions an interviewer will ask when you apply for a job, and prepare yourself for situations that you would otherwise not have expected.

You might pre-experience a date, anticipating awkward situations and skillfully manipulating matters to assure a pleasant, satisfying occasion.

Pre-experiencing is not difficult, but it does take practice in the art of giving and accepting suggestion. If you have trouble at first, I recommend that you read this chapter a second time and master the games and techniques that make them work before proceeding.

That's just a suggestion . . . but I wouldn't be surprised if you take it.

SIX

The Hypnotic Trance

We are never deceived; we deceive ourselves.
—GOETHE

The concept of an "hypnotic trance" is a myth. It's as real as the goings-on of the Greek gods on Mount Olympus. Yet it's a myth around which a cult has formed, and that makes it dangerous.

I didn't always recognize that. In fact, for nineteen years I included the sleeplike "hypnotic trance" in my concerts and TV appearances, and during that time I "hypnotized" more than thirty-five thousand people. But after some years I became first curious and then skeptical about what was really happening to produce the phenomenon everyone was calling hypnotism. Was there really a trance state? If so, what brought it about? And was the trance necessary to produce the results hypnotists claimed to achieve?

Dr. William Kroger, one of the leading medical researchers in the field, has made this enlightening statement: "It is a wise hypnotist who knows who is hypnotizing whom." Was it another case of the emperor's new clothes—the subjects unwittingly convincing the hypnotists that the hypnotic trance really exists, with no one willing to appear the fool by challenging the myth?

I began my investigation aware that, like all myths, the "hypnotic trance" is based in part on fact. Cave paintings depict humans dabbling in trances five thousand years ago. Witch doctors and medicine men used the prolonged, rhythmic beating of drums, dancing, and chanting to produce trancelike states. In Greece the cult of Aesculapius cured insomnia through apparently hypnotic trances.

Trances became significantly less popular in the Middle Ages, however, when the authorities decided they were evidence of witchcraft and burned hypnotists at the stake. It wasn't until the late 1700s that the Australian physician Franz Anton Mesmer resurrected a belief in trances, which soon became known as mesmerism.

Mesmer's stage was a mirrored hall, and his costume included flowing silk robes, a cape, and garish trappings. He was a first-class showman, but he used his talents to prey on the sick and create a large cult following. Like most cult leaders, he capitalized on a phenomenon little understood—magnetism—and built a grand theory around it.

Mesmer always performed with a steel wand. He claimed that magnetic forces controlled the health of the human body, and that by using the wand and his own power to control these magnetic forces he could drain pain and disease from the sick. While his patients sat in a magnetized circular tub, he would wave his wand, supposedly to affect the "magnetic fluids" in the ailing bodies. Within minutes his subjects would begin to shake, sometimes violently, and often scream until the "crisis" took place. Then they would go limp.

Later, because they *believed* in mesmerism, many subjects testified that they had experienced relief and apparent improvement.

Mesmer's disciples carried his work throughout Europe.

When the French physicians of Paris began losing large numbers of patients to mesmerism, a French Royal Commission conducted an investigation. Benjamin Franklin was among the scientists appointed to the inquiry board, which concluded that Mesmer's effects were purely the result of "imagination." It turned out to be a brilliantly accurate conclusion.

Some years later a student of Mesmer's, Alexander Bertrand, confirmed the finding, saying that the success was due to "imagination and suggestion."

Another mesmerist was instrumental in actually supplanting old-fashioned mesmerism with today's "hypnotic trance." One day in the 1780s a peasant boy was brought to the mesmerist the Marquis de Puysegur in hopes of relieving the child's severe headaches. Since the youngster was unschooled and untraveled, he had no idea what behavior was expected of him in response to the flamboyant gestures and waving wand, so he took the opportunity, as the pain did indeed seem to fade, to close his eyes, relax, and apparently fall asleep. Puysegur was astonished. He decided that he had discovered a totally new phenomenon.

Some forty years later, the British physician James Braid continued exploration into the "sleep trance," and gave it the name "hypnotism," from the Greek *hypnos* meaning "to put to sleep."

When Braid began his research, he announced his skepticism—and indeed he showed that Mesmer's frantic gestures, mirrors, and costume were so much hokum. What Braid *did* find was that simply by asking his subject to concentrate on a lancet or any shiny object he apparently could lead the person into a sleep state so profound that the subject actually could endure surgery without anesthesia.

We now realize that the Chinese have been doing the same for some six thousand years—through acupuncture. We have absolutely no scientific evidence that the meridians and tsubos, the points that are punctured, exist. Yet belief in acupuncture's effectiveness is universal among people of the Orient, and it's this faith that produces the result.

Braid's "hypnotism" might have played an equally important role in Western medicine but for the coincidence that
chloroform was discovered simultaneously.

Thereafter, hypnotism became the stock-in-trade of Mes-
mer-like stage magicians—which is why, even today, cartoon-
ists sometimes depict magicians with magnetic waves emanat-
ing from their fingertips. Many of these entertainers had no
concern for their subjects' physical or emotional well-being,
humiliating them by suggesting that they were all sorts of animals, and proving their lack of susceptibility to pain by burning them and sticking pins in them.

For several decades, as the stage magicians' antics grew
more outlandish, serious researchers withdrew from the field.
Only the two world wars kept alive a flicker of medical interest; army doctors discovered that such symptoms of shell
shock as amnesia and hysterical paralysis could sometimes be
relieved through hypnosis. So successful was this approach
during World War II that an upsurge in professional research
resulted.

EVERYONE BUYS
THE EMPEROR'S NEW CLOTHES

By 1955 the British Medical Association accepted hypno-
therapy as a valid field of practice, and the American Medical
Association did the same soon after. Today, 35 percent of
American medical colleges, 40 percent of graduate schools of
clinical psychology, and 30 percent of dental schools offer
courses or lectures on hypnotism. There are also several professional hypnosis societies.

Hypnosis has provided a field day for con artists, court jesters, and quacks. Example: A medium gathers the grieving into
a dark, heavily draped room, and seats them around a circular
table, holding hands. He leads them in singing hymns or
chants, then calls for silence, creating an atmosphere of high
expectation. An ethereal blue light begins to glow in a distant

corner of the room, and suddenly one of the participants whispers, "It's my dead husband!"

Example: A middle-aged woman relaxes on a couch, a well-dressed, fatherly man sitting near her. The room is dim and quiet.

"You are now in the womb," the man continues, apparently guiding her to recall memories long forgotten. "Now we will go back farther, farther. What do you remember?"

"I am in a great, open arena," the woman says in a monotone. "I see men and women, even children, huddling in the center. The gate's opening. My God—I see lions!"

Communication with the dead? Reincarnation? Not at all. These are just two examples of con men in action. That isn't to say that all of them are insincere. History is replete with people who were sincerely *wrong,* and often the first person we con is ourselves.

Nor are they examples of hypnotic trance. There were no shiny baubles dangled before the subjects' eyes, no rhythmic, monotonous murmurings. In fact, it's precisely because these effects *cannot* be explained as traditional hypnosis that they continue to lure so many people.

The court jesters I referred to earlier are the law enforcement officials who for some years now have been using "hypnotic trances" to elicit information from those who had witnessed crimes but were unable to recall pertinent details. In the past four years alone I too have assisted in the questioning of witnesses in more than eighty cases, so I'm certainly aware of the benefits of helping a witness to recall details of a crime.

The difference is that I know what I'm doing—and I'm *not* hypnotizing anyone. Few of the court jesters can say the same. Here's what can happen when the utmost care isn't taken.

• Arizona housewife Janet Buell was hypnotized in December 1980 and asked to give the license number of the burglar who had killed her husband. The police hypnotist assured her that she could see the license clearly, and she provided the number. After the session Mrs. Buell told authorities that the number she'd invented was false—she hadn't seen the car at all. Her statement checked out—there was no such license plate. Had she unwittingly given the license of someone in the neighborhood, a tragic miscarriage of justice might have occurred.

• A California man under hypnosis accused his wife of killing a two-and-one-half-year-old child. In court it was proved that he himself was the murderer.

In 1982, when the New Jersey Supreme Court was considering restrictions on hypnosis in the courts, I held a press conference on the steps of the State Supreme Court building in Trenton to demonstrate how inaccurate hypnosis can be. There were twenty-two reporters, representing CBS, Public Broadcasting Service, UPI, Associated Press, and newspapers from just about everywhere. As I interviewed a girl named Ginny, deliberately leading her as any police hypnotist might, she began trembling. A look of terror came across her face.

Ginny told me that she was lying in a hospital bed, and her father was by her side. Somehow a car had struck her while she was talking to a friend. Had she remembered an experience of her childhood? No! No such accident had ever occurred, but I had led Ginny to recall it vividly just the same.

A man who headed the chemical lobbyists in New Jersey clearly recalled being pinned against a wall by a teenage gang, and the experience was so dramatic that he began hyperventilating. If I had asked him to describe his attackers, he might well have identified innocent people, and he would have believed to his dying breath that they were guilty—*although no such attack ever took place.*

This man told the reporters later, "The false memory Kreskin suggested to me was more vivid than most of the things that have really happened to me." The reporters were stunned.

Most police hypnotists mean well, but they still think in terms of a "hypnotic trance." They ignore the subtle yet profound influences they can have in shaping a witness's recall.

Incidentally, criminals too have learned to apply the techniques of the hypnotist to their own ends by persuading themselves that they did not commit a crime of which they are, in fact, guilty. The result is that the polygraph (or lie detector), which measures blood pressure, respiration, and galvanic skin response, can sometimes indicate that they're innocent.

To lie under hypnosis, all one must do is want to lie. Simply make up your mind that you're going to lie and do it. Many courts are willing to accept anything said under hypnosis as gospel. Innocent people can be found guilty, and the guilty can go free.

During the publicity surrounding the New Jersey State Supreme Court inquiry into hypnosis in the courts I was twice approached by organized crime figures on whether it would be possible to hypnotize a group of people so that they could provide an alibi for a criminal by stating convincingly that the wrongdoer had been in their midst for an entire evening. Certainly it could be done. The man's presence would be as real and vivid to them as their own, and no polygraph or law enforcement officer or psychiatrist in the world could prove that they were lying. (The only suggestion I implanted in each case was that the gentlemen leave my hotel room.)

"Hypnosis" also has invaded virtually every branch of health care. You can receive a hypno-massage, go on a hypno-diet, visit a hypno-psychoanalyst, a hypno-gynecologist, a hypno-allergist, a hypno-chiropractor.

Perhaps the greatest sham in medicine today is the use of hypnosis in psychotherapy. At the turn of the century Freud, the founder of psychoanalysis, developed a great interest in hypnosis and experimented with it in his practice. But he dropped it like a hot rock because, he said, he discovered that his patients were *vividly misremembering*—unconsciously performing the same trick that Bridey Murphy accomplished in her reincarnation of past life experiences. His patients were unwittingly making up stories that seemed so real that both Freud and his patients were hoodwinked.

I wonder how many patients, after years of psychotherapy costing thousands of dollars, have vividly misremembered brutally incestuous relationships with father or mother, or being subjected to some horrible physical abuse. After such recall, the therapist often persuades the patient that, having discovered the source of the illness, he or she is well. I suspect that quackery and deceit on the part of the therapist is not necessarily intentional, but until mental health practitioners understand exactly what's taking place, they can't hope to guard against such mythical recall.

WHAT'S IT ALL ABOUT?

What Mesmer did, what Braid did, what the stage magician does, what doctors and police officers and mediums and psychotherapists are doing and calling hypnosis is nothing more than you learned to do in the previous chapter. *"Hypnosis" is the persuasion of a subject to accept your suggestion.*

It is not a trance. If a trance occurs, it is the *result* of an accepted suggestion. It is not a spell. It is not a form of sleep. To the extent that we respond to suggestion by others, we are all "hypnotized" every day of our lives. We meet some people who are so full of enthusiasm that they inspire us, and we accept the suggestion that whenever we're around them we'll feel inspired. Others make us feel brilliant, and somehow when we're with them we *do* behave brilliantly. Others make us feel like failures, and—we don't understand why—we stammer and make stupid remarks and behave like fools whenever we're with them. Unconsciously, we've accepted those suggestions.

In everyday conversation we use the word *suggestion* lightly, but in the context of hypnosis, I use it as a synonym for *conviction:* a secure, unwavering, and unquestioning belief.

The depth of conviction a subject can reach depends on the degree to which he manifests three qualities:

• **Imagination.** At one point during my concerts I invite fifteen or twenty volunteers to join me on the stage, quickly
determine which ones will make the best subjects, and send all
but a handful back to their seats. Then, step by step, I offer
more and more incredible suggestions: they are sweating,
they're chilly, the chairs are moving, they're talking to other
(invisible) people on the stage. Obviously, if these subjects are
too limited in imagination to recall the sensations of sweating
or shivering, they would not be capable of accepting the suggestion. Nor would they envision people who are not there.

• **Ability to concentrate.** Through many years of experience
I can now determine quickly which of the volunteers I initially
bring to the stage are really paying attention to me and which
are glancing at the audience, fidgeting, analyzing, or wandering in their thoughts. A good subject, accepting my suggestion
as conviction, will focus all of his attention on my words.

So important is concentration that a study published in the
April 1982 *American Journal of Psychiatry* showed that
psychotically ill hospital patients are significantly less capable
of accepting suggestion—or being "hypnotized," to use the
authors' term—than are normal people. The researchers concluded that "anxious preoccupation may well inhibit the concentration necessary to experience hypnosis."

•**Willingness.** An estimated 15 percent of the population
don't make good subjects for suggestion, and I believe the
main reason is that they're simply not willing to accept the
influence of another on their thoughts and behavior. That's
not to say that an experienced person can't lead even that 15
percent to accept suggestions, but it requires subtlety and
practice—and time. Unwilling people rarely make good subjects.

Of the original fifteen or twenty potential subjects who join
me onstage at the beginning of my concerts, I usually select
about six who are excellent subjects. These people will sweat
genuine perspiration on cue. They'll shiver. They'll believe
themselves floating in space—and they'll enjoy the evening
perhaps more than anyone.

FAITH-PRESTIGE

Here is the key to all I've said about con men, court jesters, quacks—and Kreskin: *The essential quality that makes suggestion work is faith-prestige.* Once that's established, the rest comes easy.

Put simply, faith-prestige is a conviction-like trust in the suggester based on the *respect the subject feels for his ability and authority.* We see faith-prestige in action every day. An elderly doctor visits his patient at the hospital and learns that drugs and attempts at encouragement by relatives have had no effect. The doctor examines the patient, names the illness, takes the patient's hand in his, reassures him that he's healing rapidly and should already begin feeling well again. The patient's face loses its lines of tension and within minutes of the doctor's departure, the formerly anxiety-ridden, emotionally tense patient relaxes in peaceful sleep.

Late at night a young woman walks along a dark alley to her home. Her mother asks why she wasn't frightened, and the woman assures her, "I saw a police officer on the way home, so I knew it was safe."

The successful medium directing a seance instills the same faith-prestige, partly through the ambiance of the room, partly through her reputation, primarily through her demeanor. Few clients would come to her in the first place if the faith-prestige relationship were not already established.

Faith-prestige can exist on a very large scale. I recall attending one of Judy Garland's last concerts at Madison Square Garden. She was in poor health at the time and arrived forty-five minutes late, obviously dazed by medication. Still a great performer, she had difficulty reaching high notes and controlling pitch. Afterward I overheard scores of people swearing she'd never sung more beautifully. Through their *imagination* they recalled the Judy Garland of years gone by. They *concentrated* on that image. And they were *willing* to believe. But it was that incredible legend's ability to establish *faith-prestige* in

I began my career as a teenager performing traditional magic. Here, a steel ball floats along a silk cloth with no apparent means of support. *(Photo credit: James J. Kriegsmann, NY)*

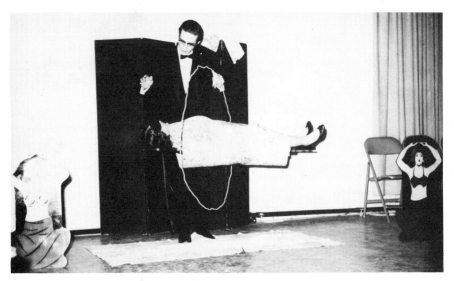

Next to pulling a rabbit out of a hat, levitation is probably the best-known of all magic illusions. Here, at age twenty-five, such effects are still an important part of my performance, although I had already spent many years experimenting with mentalism. *(Photo credit: Eric Farrar)*

Boy Scouts at the Snake River Scout Camp, Twin Rapids, Idaho, make a great audience for my ghost story. That evening I presented a $100-a-plate dinner program to help raise funds for the Scouts. *(Photo credit: Lou Freeman Earth Photography)*

At first the jumble of thoughts reaching me from the audience is chaotic. Finally, one person projects more strongly. I receive the message.

One of the great honors of my life was when Seton Hall University, in 1973, bestowed upon me an honorary Doctor of Letters degree. *(Photo credit: Van Picture Service, Inc.)*

Playing the piano started out as a favorite hobby, but as the pressures of a snowballing career increased, the keyboard also became an escape. It soothes tension and opens the door to free-flowing daydreams. *(Photo credit: Wagner International Photos, Inc.)*

When the *Courier Post* of Camden, New Jersey, advertised my debut as a newspaper columnist, they decorated almost 100 delivery trucks with these gigantic posters.

I'm with my brother, Joe Kresge, a former police officer, who now lives with his wife and two children in Florida, where he owns and manages a motel. *(Photo credit: James Young, W. Caldwell, NJ)*

On my television series, "The Amazing World of Kreskin," I had asked Rich Little to think of a dramatic incident related to his career. He was stunned when I captured the exact incident—the Sunday night when he showed up late for the Ed Sullivan TV show.

While filming my TV show in England, I asked two women to assist me. We joined hands, resting only our fingertips lightly on the table. Suddenly it lifted into the air, off the stage, and up the aisle, with us tagging along. It was no more than a traditional magic effect.

On the "Mike Douglas Show" I had just described to Soupy Sales one of his most embarrassing moments. At a time when Soupy's TV show was done live, his staff played a practical joke. Soupy opened a door on the set and found himself gazing at a naked woman. He thought the viewers were seeing her, too, but they saw only Soupy's hilarious response.

While co-hosting the "Mike Douglas Show," I was asked to play the piano, a pastime of mine that I have always concealed from my audiences. At the completion of the piece, Mike Douglas came on with the good old vaudeville hook in the spirit of the "Ted Mack Amateur Hour."

Actress Celeste Holm has just removed five cards from a deck. I asked her to think of *one* of the five cards she is holding. I don't remember if I guessed all five cards she had chosen, but I did circle the one that she had selected—and here she squealed in surprise.

I am about to ride across Louisville Downs racetrack as a promotion stunt. These frail-looking vehicles move much too fast. While I am sometimes able to control the thoughts of people, I found myself totally unable to make the horse stop. Another driver interceded.

On a rainy, dismal day in Canada, this diver submerged with a hearing device and a bag of children's blocks. My instructions to him were to think of any word in English and form the word with the blocks. He did so while at the bottom of the lake. At the same time I wrote on a large pad in front of the camera precisely the same word.

If I look relieved here, I was. Reporters had hidden my paycheck for a week of appearances at Harrah's in Reno. We were at Harrah's huge automobile museum, and the check was somewhere among those hundreds of automobiles. I finally came to a sports car, opened the door, and pulled out part of the inside lining to find my check.

I shared the stage at the Nugget nightclub in Sparks, Nevada, with its longest-running star, Bertha the elephant. Here Bertha lifts me almost to the rafters of the stage—and yet the animal proved to be one of the most gentle I've known.

Shirley Jones, appearing with me on the "Mike Douglas Show," is intrigued with a phenomenon called spontaneous telepathy, in which people become suddenly aware that loved ones are ill or in trouble. Also called the telepathic flash, it is much more common than generally realized.

Although many "extrasensory" phenomena are really examples of extreme sensitivity to the ordinary senses, I often have experiences that I cannot explain so easily. Here, I am concentrating intently. A volunteer from the audience is also concentrating on her Social Security number. In a moment I will tell her, a total stranger, the number. I would love to tell you how I do it, but I honestly don't know.

In the tube next to Mike Douglas were six blocks numbered in sequence from one to six. The great singer Enzo Stuarti also had six numbered blocks which I stacked in the random order he had been concentrating on. When I lifted the tube, the blocks in it had reorganized and were now in the same order as the blocks in front of Stuarti.

Van Johnson had in his pocket a sealed envelope I had given him at the beginning of the program—he had not seen its contents. During the program he made some apparently spontaneous decisions in situations involving a multitude of choices. When he opened the letter, it contained the very choices he had made during the program.

Although my concerts are physically exhausting—I lose as much as three pounds during a performance—I love the work. The interplay with a live audience is an emotional high. I believe I have as much fun as anyone in the house.

Sonny and Cher, co-hosting the "Mike Douglas Show" with me, expressed great interest in extrasensory perception. Sonny thought of a name, and Cher wrote down a name that came to her mentally. It was the very name that Sonny had in mind. I did this by first perceiving Sonny's thought, then mentally telegraphing it to Cher.

My good friend Virginia Graham was speechless. She had taken a deck of cards in her hands. I never touched them again. She thumbed through the deck, thought of a card, and told no one. Seconds later, with two witnesses watching, she looked through the deck. The card was gone. Standing some distance away, I asked her to rise. She had been sitting on the card!

When the New Jersey State Supreme Court was considering permitting hypnotic recall as testimony in criminal cases, I called a press conference on the courthouse steps to show that there is no such thing as hypnosis. "Hypnotism" is actually persuasion, or suggestion; the "hypnotist" can lead the suggestible witness into totally fabricated testimony. Stage hypnotists use the feat I am demonstrating here—but this man was *not* hypnotized.

the face of almost impossible odds that sold the suggestion to virtually the entire audience.

Incidentally, most people are much more susceptible to suggestion when they're part of a crowd than they would be otherwise, and the larger the crowd, the more suggestible it is. A perfect example of this is comedy. If you see a play on Broadway, you might well laugh until your sides ache, but had you seen it in a tiny off-Broadway theater—the same cast—you'd merely chuckle. Watch it at home on TV and you might never get beyond a smile. As every performer knows, whether he's a stand-up comedian, actor, or preacher, the toughest audience is the smallest one.

Part of the explanation is that the crowd response seems to validate our own feelings. If others laugh, it's all right for us to laugh too. If the masses show anger, we're justified in showing it as well. The critical analysis we usually impose on our feelings, decisions, and behavior is set aside because we accept the suggestion—reinforced by hundreds or thousands of crowd members—that a particular response is appropriate.

The result is sometimes amusing: teenagers too shy to be caught in public with a pimple scream and gyrate at a thrust of Mick Jagger's hip; people who find nothing at all funny in a comedy routine nonetheless laugh hysterically; people who have no intention of changing their lives join hundreds of others at the altar call to find God.

The hypersuggestibility of crowds also can have strikingly negative results, of course. Some years ago, a job ad brought a number of people to the vestibule of a business office where interviews were to be conducted. While quite a number of applicants sat waiting to be interviewed and a secretary worked at her desk some distance away, smoke began to seep into the room from a vent. Although the smoke was so obvious that it could hardly have been ignored by anyone in the room no one reacted. No one, apparently, wanted to counter th implied mass suggestion that it was inappropriate to point o an irregularity.

Fortunately, the entire project was a research experiment in human psychology.

It was no lab experiment, though, when millions of Americans turned their backs on the mob hysteria that led to the lynching and wounding of blacks. It was tragically real when millions of Germans built a faith-prestige relationship with Adolf Hitler and followed him to their nation's destruction. In all such cases the leader's suggestion, whether it's one of hatred, nationalistic pride, Jim Jones's religious zeal, or whatever, isn't subjected to the usual critical processes but is accepted because it's confirmed by others.

If you would identify the really dangerous person in our society, don't look for a mad scientist with his finger on the bomb, some teenage idol who tosses his clothes into the crowd, or some writer or philosopher who would lead us along a theoretical maze to embrace anarchy or communism. Look instead to the orator of the people, one in whom they have faith, one who has prestige among them. And when the masses lift him up and proclaim him their leader and follow his leading blindly—then begin to worry.

In 1970 I began to use my concerts as a research laboratory to test my theory that the hypnotic trance was simply a *manifestation* of accepted suggestion and not a *prerequisite* to it. I was taking quite a risk before my audiences, for I had been including "trances" for about twenty years, and I confess to lacking confidence that I could succeed without the crutch. As a result, I had many failures in the beginning, but eventually I learned to choose my subjects more carefully, to modify and perfect the techniques of holding my subjects' attention, establishing faith-prestige through illusion and traditional magic. Soon, at my suggestion, the subjects would freeze in awkward positions, see things that weren't there, imitate well-known entertainers, find their hands spinning. After two years I perfected the ability to implant suggestions without either subject or audience awareness—and performed every effect that had previously required a "trance."

HYPNOSIS AND THE COURTS

We're always accepting suggestion, usually for our own good. As long as the fee is reasonable, who would object to an elderly widow "communicating" with her deceased husband through a medium? Who's to say that a terminally ill cancer victim doesn't receive relief from pain—and perhaps physical benefit in the bargain—through acceptance of the suggestion that some quack drug will cure him? And if thousands sleep more peacefully and lead better lives because they believe in Bridey Murphy's reincarnation—what's wrong with that? The evil isn't with the hocus—we trip over hocus every day of our lives—but with the unscrupulous gouging of desperate victims. That's the intolerable thing.

When it comes to justice, there's less room for tolerance. I believe that the "hypnotic trance," lending itself as it does to Freud's "misremembering," should *never* be permitted as courtroom testimony. I *do* believe that it might be used to break a case when it leads to evidence that in itself will result in conviction. And I also believe that some of the techniques used in preparing a subject for suggestion can safely be used in helping a witness to recall details. For example:

The first time I assisted a police department in questioning a witness was in the early 1960s. A young woman witnessed a New Jersey bank robbery but was so upset by the experience that she developed protective amnesia. My task was similar to that of therapists treating shell-shocked soldiers during the world wars—to separate emotion from event. I led her to view the whole incident as a movie, to step back from it emotionally and just watch it happen. I helped her to relax—*but did not suggest a single detail.*

She watched the man get into the getaway car. She studied the license plate and gave the police the number. The car was found a couple of hours later and the suspects were later arrested.

In 1976 an entire busload of children and the driver were

abducted in California and buried in an underground container. Later the bus driver led the children to safety, but he was unable to describe for police the van used for the mass kidnapping. Under hypnosis he not only described the van but recalled the license number, leading to the spectacular arrest of the kidnappers. Their convictions relied on additional evidence, however.

On July 23, 1980, halfway through a performance of Stravinsky's *Firebird* at Lincoln Center a young woman violinist met the German ballerina Laura Cutler at an elevator and asked directions to the dressing rooms. When Cutler couldn't help, the man behind her offered to show the violinist the way.

The violinist failed to return for the second half of the performance and twelve hours later was found dead, apparently the victim of the man who offered her directions. Cutler could give only a very vague description until a police hypnotist worked with her. Then she vividly described for a police artist the man who, it was later discovered, was a stagehand at the theater. A month later he was found and arrested. His conviction did not rely on testimony under hypnosis but on evidence uncovered independently.

In none of these cases did the suspect's conviction rest in any way on material recalled while the witness was in a state of suggestion, although the initial breakthrough came because of it. That's crucial, because under the faith-prestige relationship that leads to effective recall, "Did the suspect have brown eyes?" can be interpreted by the subject as "The subject *did* have brown eyes."

"Was this the man you saw?" can mean to the cooperating subject, eager to please, "This was the person, wasn't it?" An eager investigator might tell a witness she saw a car, and the witness will cooperate by describing one. It's not impossible that a subject who always "knew" that his neighbor was dishonest will unconsciously persuade himself that he saw the neighbor commit a crime.

Some of those problems can be avoided if the investigator will simply stop thinking of himself as a *hypnotist,* charged with inducing trances or semisleep states, and recognize instead his function as an *interviewer*. Using basic techniques of relaxation and concentration, he should try to release the subject from the tensions associated with the event. Once relaxation is established, he should help the subject to visualize the scene. But he should contribute not a single detail.

For example, he should *not* say, "Do you hear the horns?" Instead he should say, "Listen, what sounds do you hear?"

In 1981 Arizona and Minnesota banned all evidence obtained by hypnosis, and challenges to testimony are being fought in the courts of six other states. In March of 1982 the California Supreme Court also banned virtually all witnesses who had been hypnotized from giving evidence in court. The judges ruled that hypnotized persons often produce "pseudo memories or fantasies" that they later insist are true.

A wise jurist once said, "I would rather a hundred guilty men go free than one innocent be condemned." In that light I hope we'll one day see all testimony obtained under hypnosis prohibited in courts.

SEVEN

Nature and
Human Nature

All knowledge must be built on our intuitive beliefs . . .
—BERTRAND RUSSELL, The Problems of Philosophy

In the early days of television Mike Wallace, now of "60 Minutes" fame, launched his reputation as a hard-hitting inquisitor on a show called "Night Beat." He interviewed politicians and other controversial figures, questioning and often badgering them mercilessly.

I doubt that Wallace's "Night Beat" "victims" realized it, but the host stacked the cards against them even before the show began. He used subtle but profoundly effective techniques.

First, Wallace had the guest sit in what appeared to be an old school chair with a single arm that flared to form a writing surface. The chair itself suggested a child-teacher relationship, with Wallace being the authority figure. The smallness of the chair added a sense of confinement that physically—and therefore psychologically and verbally—restricted the guest.

But the real clincher was a simple glass of water placed on that writing surface a few inches from the guest. It was Wallace's supreme weaponry, for the slightest careless gesture on the guest's part could send it crashing to the floor, making him or her look like a clumsy baboon. The result was that while Wallace could verbally slash the guest at will, the guest could not feel so free and spontaneous with his emotions.

Without uttering a word Wallace said to his guests: "I'm the authority figure; you're a virtual child. I'm free to attack; you're to remain restrained."

Each of us deals with people every day on this level of wordless communication. We make wordless statements and commands. We hear wordless comments. And insofar as we become adept at this voiceless language, we can anticipate another's behavior—sometimes even before the person himself decides on it—and we can adapt accordingly.

For example, you can produce an effect similar to Wallace's with an ordinary pad and pencil. Whenever the person you're interviewing makes a statement, scribble something on the pad. It needn't have anything to do with what's being said— you can write the word *elephant* repeatedly. Whatever you write should be brief, giving the impression that you have summarized several of your subject's sentences in just a few words. Then return your gaze to the speaker.

That must stimulate some incompletely formed questions in the subject's mind: Am I talking too much? Should I be more concise? Is she writing not about what I'm saying but the way I'm sitting—or the way I'm dressed? Is she finding fault with my ideas? In a matter of minutes the subject can be so intimidated and self-conscious as to seem almost foolish.

In fact, Freud recognized in the early days of his practice that his patients actually became fixated on his pad and pencil. He might jot down a note having nothing to do with what a patient said, but in the patient's mind Freud's writing gave whatever statement the patient happened to have made at the moment enormous significance. It's for that reason that the analyst now sits behind the patient, where he can't be seen.

Demian, the title character in the Hermann Hesse novel, had mastered the ability to "read" people to the amazement of his friend, who asked him,

"Can you actually make someone think what you want him to?" He answered readily in his quiet, factual and adult manner.

"No," he said, "I can't do that. . . . However, one can study someone very closely and then one can often know almost exactly what he thinks or feels and then one can also anticipate what he will do the next moment. It's simple enough, only people don't know it. Of course you need practice."

In this chapter we're going to follow Demian's example and study each other very closely—both some little-known functions of our minds and also those of our bodies. We will learn just a few of the thousands of conversations we have with each other every day—without speaking a word. And we'll learn how we can utilize these effects to entertain in our living rooms and to improve our daily lives.

First, allow me to dash your hopes if you're looking forward to a list of subtle keys to reading people's minds: one raised eyebrow—doubt; two raised eyebrows—surprise; both eyebrows lowered—distrust.

That popular approach may appeal superficially, but it's about as scientific as measuring the bumps on a person's head in the field of phrenology to determine intelligence. Just as oral communication is more than mere words—inflection, pauses, volume, and much more are essential to verbal communication —so wordless language is more than translating a series of gestures. Analyzing one or two won't give you the answer and will probably produce a mistaken conclusion.

Just such a mistake almost lost me several thousand dollars some years ago. I had an appointment with a well-known show producer in New York City, and it was an important opportunity for me. His secretary ushered me into the largest office I'd ever seen, yet it was almost barren of furniture. At the far end of the room the producer sat behind an elevated and imposing desk. At his back, as well as to the left, floor-to-ceiling windows displayed a brilliant skyline and the glaring afternoon sun. He stood, shook my hand, and gestured to the chair in front of his desk. I practically had to peer over the desk to see his head. His features were lost in shadow.

We had come to talk money, and there was quite a gap between what he had offered and what I wanted. Yet as the conversation got underway, it became apparent that he was in control. Suddenly I understood why. The sun, glaring in my face, had distracted me just as it does a crime suspect when he's being questioned under bright lights. I had been put on the defensive, and the difference in our physical positions—he towering over me from behind the fortress of his desk—didn't help matters.

"Forgive me, my legs are stiff and I prefer to stand," I told him, walking casually toward the windows to his left. Turning to face him, my back to the window, I said, "Please go on."

I folded my arms—my own fortress—and tightened my lips to show my resolve.

The poor fellow actually stammered. I noticed he began shaking his foot, not so cool after all. His eyes darted from my face to the floor to his hands. Now the sun behind me was blinding *him*.

We resolved the question with a compromise not much below my original asking price and precisely the amount I'd determined to settle for long before the meeting. Had I been content to read only the obvious wordless messages—the strength of his handshake, the coolness of his voice, his apparent unassailable position—it would have cost me a bundle.

LISTENING TESTS

The all-time master of wordless communication is probably Sir Arthur Conan Doyle's fictional detective Sherlock Holmes. In "A Case of Identity" Holmes watches while an elaborately dressed woman "peeped up in a nervous, hesitating fashion at our windows, while her body oscillated backward and forward, and her fingers fidgeted with her glove buttons. Suddenly, with a plunge, as of a swimmer who leaves the bank, she hurried across the road and we heard the sharp clang of the bell.

" 'I have seen those symptoms before,' said Holmes, throwing his cigarette into the fire. 'Oscillation upon the pavement always means an *affaire de coeur*. She would like advice, but is not sure that the matter is not too delicate for communication. And yet even here we may discriminate. When a woman has been seriously wronged by a man, she no longer oscillates, and the usual symptom is a broken bell wire. Here we may take it that there is a love matter, but that the maiden is not so much angry as perplexed, or grieved.' "

The following tests won't lead to such an intricate understanding of nature and human nature, but they'll give you insights that will astonish you and your friends. Indeed, some are so amazing that your friends will believe—correctly—that you've read their minds.

THE GREEDY EYE

Ask a volunteer to sit in a straight-back chair while you sit in another facing him, your knees almost touching. Show him four small sheets of paper or three-by-five cards. Allow him to examine them if he wishes. Take back the cards and, while he and your audience watch, draw a large dollar sign on one of the cards. Hand them back to the volunteer.

You must now erect a visual barrier between your eyes and your subject's hands. A large serving tray works well, as does a small chair cushion. For a more dramatic effect, you might have two more volunteers hold a towel between you and the subject. *It must not be raised so high as to interfere with your view of the subject's face.*

Now say:

"I want you to concentrate on the one thing you would most like to own—something that money can buy. What is the one object you would like to own? Don't answer—just envision it. Picture it clearly in every detail."

Give your subject ten or fifteen seconds to follow your instructions. Then explain:

"We're going to pretend that all the money you need to buy the object you just envisioned can be *yours* tonight. The card with the *dollar sign* represents that money, and it can be *yours* —unless I can identify the card as you look upon it. I want you to shuffle the cards and put them into any order you like."

When the cards are shuffled, explain that the order can no longer be changed; if you think your volunteer has a shady nature, appoint an observer to guarantee that your instructions are followed. Now say:

"Please study the first card carefully. Keep looking at it. Now look at me."

Tell him to put the top card—now called card number one —on the bottom. Follow the same procedure with each of the four cards. Perhaps you will ask the volunteer to reexamine one or two of the cards, then to look up into your eyes— quickly.

Finally, sit back and announce: "The card with the dollar sign is the third one you originally looked at." (Or the first, second, or fourth.)

I have seen people turn white in astonishment at the thought that I've read their minds. And of course they're correct. That's just what I—and you—have done. Or to be a bit more precise, we've listened to a wordless communication that told us what was in the mind.

The key is the *pupil of the volunteer's eye*. That introductory business about imagining the object you would like most to own if you had the money is not polite chit-chat—it's a method of giving real *value* to that little card with the dollar sign scrawled on it. To the volunteer that card becomes the gateway, through his imagination, to a lifelong dream.

As the volunteer peers first at one of the three blank cards, then into your eyes, you'll note little if any change in the size of the pupil of his eye. When he gazes at the card with the dollar sign, however, you'll see a much more noticeable change. His pupil will dilate as he looks at the card—but you won't notice that, for he will be glancing downward, and his pupils will be covered by his eyelids. As he lifts his head and looks into your eyes, the overhead light—which should be no brighter than necessary for you to see his pupils—might cause the pupils to grow momentarily smaller, but even that movement tells you that they had been larger. As they adjust, they will grow large again.

The change occurs to varying degrees, depending on individual sensitivity. But *any* change is a good indicator. If you aren't certain of the reading, ask the volunteer to reexamine the cards you suspect.

Here are two points to keep in mind:

Continue to reinforce the importance of the dollar sign as the volunteer views each card.

Allow him to gaze at each card for only a few seconds so that you can observe the pupil as it begins to dilate. In some subjects the response is relatively brief.

The pupil dilation phenomenon was once tested in a scientific study that offers interesting possibilities. Researchers discovered that when subjects were shown ordinary photographs of landscapes, houses, and other nonemotional subjects, their pupils did not change. When they were shown sexually oriented photographs involving members of the opposite gender, however, their pupils dilated dramatically. The next time you want to know if an attractive individual is interested in a more intimate relationship, you might study the person's pupils as you make subtly suggestive remarks.

Most professional card players already know that pupils can tip off even the most "poker faced" opponent's hand. When the pro sees dramatically dilated pupils across the table, he will seriously consider throwing in his cards. If the pupils remain small, yet the opponent continues to raise the bid, it's probably a bluff.

Oriental dealers of expensive merchandise are often trained to watch a customer's eyes to see when he is sufficiently ex-

cited by an object to risk asking a very high price. The salesman today might take a lesson from his Oriental counterparts.

SPOTTING THE LIE

I always make it a point to involve the audience as much as
possible in my concerts, for it not only goes a long way toward
establishing the faith-prestige relationship, but also creates a
partylike atmosphere that's much more fun for the audience
and myself. One of the most popular audience participation
effects is SPOTTING THE LIE. Here's how it's done:

Select five people from among your party guests. (If the
group is small, choose three.) If there are enough guests, try to
select volunteers that are hyperresponsive—the sort who laugh
first and longest, applaud enthusiastically, gasp in surprise.

Announce to the guests, including the subjects:

"I have here five marbles. As you can see, four of them are
white, one is black. I'm going to wrap each marble in alumi-
num foil and drop it into this brown bag. Each volunteer will
take a marble from the bag and unwrap it privately—only he
will know the color of the marble he has selected.

"I'll question each volunteer. When I'm through, we'll all
vote on who is holding the black marble in his or her hand."

If you don't have five marbles, you can use coins just as well
—four quarters and one half dollar will work well. After the
selections have been made and each subject has had a chance
to examine his marble or coin, say:

"Now, I have *given* the white marbles [or quarters] to four
of these people, but I did not give the black marble away. The
black marble was *stolen*. One of these five people is a *thief,* and
the evidence is in that person's hand at this moment. Will the
five subjects please be seated."

After they've taken their seats facing the party guests, stare
into each face. Then begin the questioning with the first suspect. Invent your own questions, along these lines:

"Do you find black marbles attractive? If you wanted it,
why didn't you buy it? You stole it, didn't you? Why didn't

you just ask for it—why did you feel you had to steal it? You have it there in the palm of your hand right now, don't you—the black marble?"

(Incidentally, all subjects should be instructed to deny having the black marble, and no one, including you, should know which volunteer has it, except the guilty person.)

After you've interviewed all the subjects thoroughly, put the question to a vote according to the number of the chair in which the five volunteers are sitting. It can be a paper ballot tabulated by one of the guests, or the vote can be by raised hands. You should cast your own vote in writing, but keep your choice secret until the audience has voted.

Chances are, the guilty suspect will be convicted unanimously. The nature of the wordless confession will vary from subject to subject, but it will be so obvious that even those untrained in the field will recognize the signs when they appear: excessive shifting of posture, nervous fidgeting, clenching of the hand holding the marble, an exaggerated effort to appear casual contradicted by vocal stress, giggling, a tapping foot, and so forth. Although most of us do it unconsciously, we all listen to this silent language every day in deciding whether or not to trust and believe other people, from newscasters to salesclerks.

THE NOISY HANDSHAKE

When I shake a person's hand, I do so with such enthusiasm that Mike Douglas said it reminded him of someone milking a cow. I try to convey several messages with that handshake—although you must understand that the messages, like the handshake itself, are spontaneous and are as natural to me as breathing. I want the people I meet to realize that it's not just "good" to meet them, as we say so often, but I consider it a really exciting experience. I want them to realize that I'm "up" on life and that I'm energetic and that energy can be contagious. Millions of people feel exactly as I do, I'm sure, but I think many of them are constrained somewhere between their shoulders and elbows—the enthusiasm never flows into their handshakes. I allow the wordless communication to flow. Unless the other fellow has a painful wrist or stiff arm, the result is always positive.

I'm talking here about listening to the silent communication of others, and you can hear a lot in a handshake. In fact, simply by shaking the hands of guests at a party or volunteers on the stage, you can go a long way toward determining which people will make the best subjects later.

The Cooperative Handshake

Usually, the ideal subject will grip my hand firmly. Although he or she is often momentarily surprised by the energy of my own shake, the good subject will relax and match it. The unspoken message: "I want to cooperate; you lead and I'll follow." The firmness indicates that they're not passive. I can expect them to participate in an active, imaginative way. That will make the effect more entertaining.

The Resisting Handshake

There are those who simply "put on the brakes" before the handshake even gets underway. The message is as clear as if they had actually spoken it: "Let's keep this a formal, nonemotional relationship." Such a person has no intention of going with the flow and will probably simply refuse to be a subject. If he does agree, he'll resist suggestion—although his frustration will be very obvious, and entertaining, when he fails some of the tests in the chapter "You're Stronger Than You Think."

The Dynamo Handshake

Occasionally I come across people who try to outshake even me. They're usually strong, burly men or highly successful women, people confident of their own abilities, yet outgoing and fond of their fellow human beings. Whenever I receive such a handshake, I know that I'm meeting either the best subject in the room or the most challenging skeptic, depending upon how I deal with the person. The handshake is saying, *"I should be the one getting the attention here. I'm the leader."* But it also says, "It's important to me that things get done and get done right, and I enjoy cooperating toward that end." Subtle, but not false, flattery can be very effective in winning the allegiance of the dynamo. If you want his cooperation later, don't use him in tests where people will laugh at his failure.

The Limp Handshake

A lifeless handshake can have several meanings, and you must go beyond the handshake itself to determine which is the correct one. It might mean that the individual is ill, depressed, or distracted, all of which make the subject less than ideal. It might indicate shyness, and an excessively self-conscious subject isn't a good one. It might indicate a lack of interest or even a surly distaste for you personally or the effects you'll later perform. And of course it could indicate that the person has a genuinely passive nature, willing to do whatever is required but with little enthusiasm or interest.

You'll need some way to determine exactly what a particular limp handshake means, since you might want a passive, cooperative volunteer and get stuck with a hostile one if you're not careful. One approach is to listen to additional unspoken communication. Folded arms, tight lips, a raised chin all suggest that you're being shut out or rejected. Taken together, they make a pretty loud statement. When only one condition exists, there can be so many other possible reasons for it that you shouldn't put much faith in that interpretation.

You can also use a direct question to clarify the handshake's meaning: "Have you ever performed professionally?" Here are some self-explanatory responses you might get:

"My goodness, no!" (With giggles and falling gaze.)

"I think performers are rather immature."

"Where would I get so much energy?"

I'll talk later about some additional behavior patterns that broadcast what we are thinking.

The tests I've discussed until now are *listening* tests in which you "hear" things people didn't know they were telling you. But there's another side to every conversation, including the silent ones, and it's possible to have people respond without their knowledge to your silent commands. Here's an example:

In October of 1982 I was performing in Boca Raton, Florida, when I met a reporter who had just written a fine story about my work for the local paper. I invited him, his wife, and daughter backstage after a concert one night, and we talked about my views on the myth of the hypnotic trance, the role of suggestion, and finally of implanting a suggestion—giving a command—wordlessly. I saw that he was skeptical.

"I wonder—is your newspaper part of the Gannett chain?" I asked. "I write a weekly column for a Gannett paper in Camden, New Jersey."

"No," he began, "we're with . . ."

As he spoke, I slapped him lightly on the shoulder. "With what?" I asked.

"With . . . with . . ." He couldn't recall the name of the company that owned his own newspaper!

"It's on the tip of my tongue," he stammered, a look of absolute bafflement on his face.

"Yes, but you just can't think of it." His amnesia continued for about thirty seconds, while his wife and daughter looked on incredulous.

I snapped my fingers—and the name came to him immediately. I had illustrated my point: that people can be influenced to accept a command given without words.

That particular feat, incidentally, is very difficult to accomplish and luck must be on your side. There is usually just an instant as you ask a question when the responder has not yet formulated an answer. That instant might actually be before you have finished asking the question, for we speak at only one hundred twenty words per minute, but we listen and think in excess of five hundred words per minute. During that instant between the time your listener understands where the question is going and the formulation of his response, any unexpected event can leave his mind a blank. My tap on the shoulder did the trick. I followed it up instantly with the suggestion that he could not, in fact, recall the name. He accepted the suggestion, and his mind remained blank until I gave him reason to feel released.

While that effect is pretty difficult, requiring several years of practice, you can achieve some very impressive effects yourself through silent commands and a knowledge of human nature.

CHOOSE THE OBJECT

Although you will speak during this effect, your words alone will not produce success. It's the *unspoken* command that will convince both subject and audience that you've actually entered into people's minds and programmed their response.

And that's exactly what you will do.

Pass out a pencil and small piece of paper to each of three volunteers. Say:

"I'm going to place five objects on this table. One is a coin." Take a coin from your pocket and place it on the table. "The second is this pen." Take a gold or silver pen from your pocket, and before placing it on the table, point it to each of the subjects. While you are pointing it, say: "I want you to *concentrate* on each of these objects." Casually lay the pen next to the coin.

Add three other objects—a matchbook, tie clip, and wallet will do. As you place the objects, continue to talk about the need for emptying the mind of outside influence—but don't mention the word *concentrate*.

Pick up the coin and show it to the volunteers, again urging them to observe it carefully. Place it on the table and pick up the pen. Say:

"Please *concentrate*. The entire key is that you *concentrate*."

Place the pen on the table. Lift up the remaining objects one by one, asking your subjects to examine them carefully. Now give these instructions:

"Please take three steps back. Raise the paper and be prepared to write immediately. I want you to write the very first object on the table that comes to your mind. Now! *Concentrate!*"

At the same time, you write the word *pen* on a slip of paper.

At least two out of three—and probably all of the volunteers—will write the same word you've written. When each of the guests shows the object they have selected and you show that it's the same object you've chosen to impress on their minds, everyone, including the participants, will be astonished. The key, of course, is that you issued a subtle silent command. Every time you used the word *concentrate,* you casually lifted the pen and pointed it at the subjects. When you ordered them to write immediately without thinking, using the word *concentrate* again immediately, you were as much as telling them to write the word *pen.*

The ways in which you might apply that basic principle of the silent command are innumerable. Greet someone at the party with your hand upraised as though cutting the air, and, all things being equal, your acquaintance will come to greet you. If you turn your palm toward him in the same salute, the police officer's classic stop signal, there's every likelihood he'll unconsciously recognize that command and merely return the greeting but not approach.

Handling any object, even glancing repeatedly at it, will give it special significance in the minds of those who observe you. You can sometimes subtly relate that object to another factor with startling effects. Here's what I mean:

Some years ago Jeff Carpenter, formerly with Roy Clark's organization, became my road manager. We were dining at a restaurant during a tour one evening with a third man, a promoter, when we realized that Jeff knew someone who could prove the key figure in arranging a series of important appearances. We all grew very excited. There was just one small problem—Jeff couldn't remember the man's name!

We quizzed him. We prompted him. We begged him. Jeff grew more and more forlorn.

"All right, Jeff, put it aside," I said finally. "It will come to you later on." Jeff was a drinker of milk, and while I talked about how useless it was to make a conscious effort to recall forgotten details, I toyed with that glass of milk, keeping my eyes on it.

Finally, I took my hand from the glass and said, "Jeff, this will seem like a silly request, and I don't wish to explain it now, but I would prefer if you don't touch that glass of milk until after dessert."

Jeff is a quiet, friendly man who at that time was quite used to my antics. He smiled, shrugged, and said, "Okay, Kreskin."

Nothing more was said of either the name or the milk, but at a moment somewhere between the tossed salad and rack of lamb, Jeff, without giving it a thought, reached for the milk and brought it to his lips.

"What's the name of that person we need for this deal?" I asked him.

And with no more fanfare than if I had asked him his own name, he told me.

What really happened? My *silent* command to Jeff was to associate the milk with the name. Sipping the milk throughout the meal was one of Jeff's unconscious habits, dictated by neither thirst nor any other conscious need. When the unconscious urge to reach for the milk came to the surface, it brought the name with it.

A young college graduate once told me, "I started my freshman year thinking I knew everything, and I finished my senior year convinced I knew just about nothing." That fellow received a fine education.

As the proverb has it, "He that knows nothing, and knows he knows nothing, knows much."

Much of our society today is in the freshman class. We have

all the answers. We think we *know* there is *no God.* We think we *know* the truth about man's origins. We surely know what's right and wrong with the way our neighbors behave. And of course we know the truth about man himself—that he is a mechanistic functioning of interrelated molecules, the responses of which are predictable through an understanding of genetic components.

Well, I *don't* know all that, and while I can understand and even admire the doubter who seriously seeks the truth, I've little patience with the fellow who *knows* the answers to questions few people can even *ask* properly.

I suppose that this headstrong, self-satisfied phase is as natural for a society contemplating new thoughts and learning astonishing new information daily as it is for that college freshman, but I for one am growing weary of it and look with eagerness toward graduation day.

The origin of man! We don't even know the origin of insomnia, schizophrenia, manic depression. We don't know the difference, in measurable, chemical terms, between anger and ecstasy. I suspect that only freshmen are prepared to make final pronouncements regarding ultimate questions.

In these pages we've learned a few little-known facts about human nature, and I hope it's been a source of good fun. But I'd like to think it's been a humbling experience, too, as it is for me, for it's a mere suggestion of all that we do *not* know about ourselves and each other. Let's continue with one of the world's best-known "supernatural" phenomena.

THE TILTING TABLE

I've placed "supernatural" in quotes because the medium at whose seances this spectacular effect sometimes occurs tends to explain it as a manifestation of spirits from the hereafter (or thereafter, or wherever). It is no such metaphysical sideshow.

Nor is it the trickery of a scheming con artist. There are no hidden wires, magnets or springs.

In fact, it's a perfectly natural occurrence, and you can

reproduce it right now just as I have on the "David Frost Show," Johnny Carson's stage, and my own television show.

Use a light but sturdy card table, with one volunteer sitting at each of the four sides. The table must be on a wood or linoleum floor—definitely not carpet. Instruct the volunteers as follows:

"Place your hands palms down about six inches from the edge facing you and close enough to the outer edges so that your little fingers are touching the little fingers of the people to your right and left. Be sure that you maintain this contact, for it establishes the dynamic force field that is essential.

"Now, press *firmly* on the table and concentrate."

Don't expect immediate results if this is your first attempt—it takes a great deal of practice to select the best volunteers and implant the subtle suggestion that leads to the immediate responses produced at my concerts. Perhaps it will take only a few minutes when you try it with a few seriously interested friends (don't waste time with those not interested, since it might take as much as thirty minutes to get a response). The table *will* move—actually slide across the floor for a few inches —and when it does, you'll know it was worth waiting for.

The table-tilting effect has often been the most entertaining aspect of a performance. With one volunteer stepping aside, a table once fell into an orchestra pit. (On stage, I always have participants stand—the results are more dramatic.) Another plunged against the rear curtain backdrop with the volunteers still standing around it. Another card table seemed to have a mind of its own. It refused to move—just kept collapsing.

I used four tables on the "David Frost Show," and two of them actually flipped over. Frost himself was so intrigued that he extended my segment to question the participants. Several explained that their hands went numb. A man said that "electricity was in the table," and a girl said she "felt moving water on the table top."

In fact, table tilting is an entirely natural phenomenon (akin incidentally, to that of the Ouija board, which I'll discuss in a later chapter). It's caused by a combination of neuromuscular responses to concentration, and muscle fatigue. Suggestion can speed the results, but is definitely not essential. Muscular effort required of any one individual to move the table is so minimal that the person himself is not aware of his involuntary contribution to the effect. But like the four men who lifted a woman using just two fingers each, the *combined* response of the volunteers can have dramatic effects. Usually, no one is more startled than the participants themselves.

LIGHTER THAN AIR

Here's another effect based on a natural function of our bodies. You can test it yourself right now.

Stand in a narrow doorway, your arms at your sides. Now, keeping your arms straight, press the backs of your hands against the door frame with *all* your strength, as though you're Samson trying to collapse the columns of the temple. Looking straight ahead, count slowly to yourself from one to ten.

At the final count, step forward into the room, away from walls and furniture, and you'll find your arms rising like an elevator, perhaps to shoulder level, entirely without asking your permission!

If the effect is only minimal, you probably weren't pressing with all your strength, or you counted too fast.

This makes an amusing parlor game, particularly with a suggestible subject. Instruct the volunteer to stand erect in the doorway and press both hands outward against the frame while watching your hands carefully. Say:

"Keep pressing out . . . outward . . . outward . . . harder, harder." While talking, tense your own arms and hands and raise them slightly upward. Say:

"Keep watching my hands . . . watch . . . watch . . ."

After at least ten seconds have passed, instruct the volunteer to step forward. As he does, raise your arms slowly toward shoulder level and observe:

"Your arms are lighter than air, aren't they?"

The volunteer will probably giggle with surprise and minor

embarrassment as, without the slightest conscious effort on his part, his arms float upward.

You can perform this effect with as many as four people at the same time by having them stand with one side facing a heavy table. Have each press the back of one hand against the side of the table as you repeat the words above. After ten seconds, ask them to turn and face the opposite direction as you sweep your own hands upward. Make sure you position them so that when they turn around, they can all see your arms rising.

Some years ago a well-known stage hypnotist used this effect to prove that his subjects were "hypnotized." He would have them step away from a door frame and, by sweeping his own arms upward, persuade both subject and audience that the volunteer was obeying in robot-fashion his silent command. In fact, the subject's muscles were simply continuing to contract as they had been when pressing the hands against the door frame—a brief, lingering "memory" of nervous stimulation to the cells.

The following effects illustrate a few of the many limitations nature places on us, limitations few of us are aware of. Once again, they illustrate just how much we don't know, even about ourselves, and the perfect patsy for these effects is the individual who still thinks he knows everything. On occasion a volunteer will go so far as to want to wager that you can't fool him.

A fool and his money are soon parted, as Benjamin Franklin observed.

CLICKING COINS

Many people are quick to be skeptical when dealing with instinctual or emotional truths, yet they'll vest unwavering faith in the five senses. We've found repeatedly in these pages that the senses can't always be trusted, and here's another effect to prove the point.

Bring your volunteer to the middle of the room and show him and your guests two coins—quarters will do. Ask everyone to be silent and tap one coin against the other so that all can hear the sound. Say to the volunteer:

"I want you to close your eyes. I'm going to tap these coins in various areas around you. I want you to point to the direction you think the sound is coming from."

Proceed to do that, standing first beside him, then in front, in back. After each tap of the coins, have him first point to where the sound is coming from, then open his eyes and check his own accuracy. He'll probably prove rather accurate during this phase, so announce, "Some guests might think that you're peeking just a little, so to prove them wrong I'm going to blindfold you." While one person is applying the blindfold, explain that the volunteer will now have to make a greater effort to tell whether the sound is in front of him, on either side, or behind him. While you're talking, reach for a nearby chair and bring it close to the volunteer. It must be a sturdy one that will not creak. As you continue to walk around him so that he gets used to hearing your voice from all four directions, explain:

"From now on, I won't speak to you. I'll merely tap the coins, and you'll respond by telling me that I'm to your left, right, in front, or behind. You'll respond after each click of the coins."

Now, quietly mount the chair and click the coins about two feet above his head. If he doesn't respond after a few seconds, click again and have an assistant instruct him to name the direction the sound came from.

Chances are he'll point to every direction at least once but never point above him. The louder the guests laugh, the more baffled he'll become. To conclude, you might ask him to point in the direction he believes the final click came from and to continue pointing while the blindfold is removed.

THE IMMOVABLE KNEE

Your success with this effect will rely on one of the most fundamental principles of nature—gravity—and on your ability to successfully persuade your subject to believe otherwise. Ask your volunteer to stand with his feet about ten inches apart and not to move his feet until you tell him to. Standing at his right side, reach across him to brush his left knee with your hand. Explain:

"There are certain delicate nerves extending from your upper thigh muscles, the quadriceps, into the kneecap. Although it's not widely known, these nerves can freeze the knee joint." As you talk, massage the tendons above the kneecap, squeezing sufficiently so that the volunteer feels the pressure and begins to wonder if what you say is true. Continue to explain that you're now stimulating those nerves and the knee joint is actually locked. Say:

"Now, slowly, try to bend your knee and lift your left foot from the floor."

He won't be able to do it!

Tell him to cease all efforts, reach across him to brush the tendons in the opposite direction, step in front of him and order him to lift the foot from the floor. This time he'll succeed.

His knee had nothing to do with it, of course. To lift his left foot, he had to transfer the center of his body's gravity over his right foot. That means shifting his hip to the right. However, you make that impossible, for while you are calling attention to his knee, you are standing so close to his right hip that you prevent him from shifting his weight. When taking your position, place your left foot almost against his right foot. After you've "frozen" his knee, stand with your hip and shoulder almost touching him. As long as you keep his attention on his knee, he'll never guess what's actually happening.

To prepare for this effect, rehearse it alone first by standing sideways with your right foot against the baseboard of a wall, your feet ten inches apart. Then try to lift your left foot. You won't succeed because the wall prevents you from shifting your hip to the right.

You can also use the wall instead of your body with a volunteer, persuading him that it's that nerve in his knee rather than the wall that's causing him the problem.

To me the most fascinating thing about understanding the subtleties of human nature is in being able to understand the "conversation within the conversation." *Every one of us* converses on two levels—the *verbal* and the *functional.* We communicate by both what we say and what we do. Sometimes our gestures and expressions amplify and complement our words. Sometimes they deny or contradict them.

In modern society no survival tool is more important than this ability to read wordless communication. Yet I would find it easier to teach people how to express themselves fluently in Chinese (which I don't speak, incidentally) than to teach them wordless communication.

Every day we make statements, raise questions, propose alternatives, and insist on our point of view thousands of times without ever speaking a word. We tighten our lips to express anger, use gestures in speech that include part of a group while rejecting another part, show decisiveness with chopping motions, magnanimity with open arms, palms outward. We tell strangers on the subway we're not interested in conversing by crossing the leg nearest to them over the opposite one and turning our backs. We avoid confrontation by dropping our eyes, and we show interest and respect by gazing eyeball to eyeball.

We announce what we want other people to think of us by the clothes we wear. A dark three-piece suit obviously means "I want you to think of me as dignified." A casual blazer says, "I'm a good old sport," and an expensive one is the property of a man who sees himself as a playboy, a man of the world. Tattered clothes worn by someone who can afford better is a neon sign saying, "I have the courage to reject the establishment's values." Low neckline and high skirt: "I want you to think I'm sexually attractive." Neatly tailored but basically shapeless outfit: "I am *first* of all intelligent."

If you would learn wordless communication for yourself— and there is no other way—realize first that everything about another person is a continuing series of statements. And that's true of you as well. What you wear says something. How you sit, walk, gesture, smile, frown, are all part of the eloquent language beyond words. When you realize that, you will begin looking for it, listening to it.

From that point it's a small step to consciously framing those silent statements you make to others, forming the opinions about you that are in your best interest and perhaps theirs as well.

EIGHT

The Educated Guess

*To know a little less and to understand a little more: that, it
seems to me, is our greatest need.*
—JAMES RAMSEY ULLMAN, The White Tower

On April 2, 1965, I made four predictions that gained widespread coverage, and in spite of my denials, they led some to
claim that I was a "seer" or prophet. I was appearing at the
Weldwood Lounge, a nightclub near Scranton, Pennsylvania,
and for publicity purposes I told a gathering of newspaper,
radio, and TV reporters what I thought the front page story
would be in the Scranton *Tribune* exactly a week later—on
April 9.

Actually, I made three predictions and would have taken
my bow had any one of them proved accurate.

The first: "Collision Kills Driver, Demolishes Car. A
twenty-two-year-old man or woman will be involved."

The second: "Robber in Gun Battle with Police."

The third: "Eighteen-year-old Negro Terrorized."

I added one qualifier: "The car crash tragedy may be pushed

off the front page by the Health-Welfare Bill vote. If so, the House of Representatives will pass it by approximately two hundred votes."

The following week the headline on page one read, "City Man Dies in Car Crash." Beneath that: "Small Foreign Car Demolished." The victim was a twenty-two-year-old man.

Another story on the front page was titled, "Robber in Store Holds Off Police Three Hours."

The main story was: "Arrest 2 Cops for Terrorizing Negro."

Finally—also on page one—the news that the House had passed the Health-Welfare measure by 198 votes.

I have made similar "prophecies" many times in the almost twenty years since then, often before millions of TV viewers. One of the most astonished witnesses I can remember was Joey Bishop, when I predicted the stories that would appear in the *Los Angeles Times.* On the air a Los Angeles police detective opened the envelope in which the predictions had been sealed. My prediction was accurate almost word for word. So was the subject matter of the editorial page. We were baffled when the story on nerve gas—my final prediction—could not be located in either of the paper's first two editions. Fortunately, during a station break someone brought us the *Times*'s final edition, and we found the nerve-gas story on page five.

I confess that although my batting average through the years has surpassed that of Jeane Dixon and other well-known "seers," a number of my predictions have failed. The public tends to remember the accurate forecasts and forget the failures, partly because those who make them promote their successes exhaustively. The difference between many of them and me is that I make no claims to mystical powers. I'm entirely willing to confess that my predictions are nothing more than educated guesses.

Take those predictions in Scranton, Pennsylvania, for example. In a city that size fatal accidents are, tragically, commonplace. Yet I hedged my bet by not stating that the accident would occur in Scranton—it might have happened in Wilkes-Barre, or the victim might have been a Scranton resident killed in an accident anywhere. Giving the victim's age was a shot in the dark based on the fact that most accident victims are young. A miss would have been ignored; as it was, the bull's-eye made me look very good indeed.

A robber in a gun battle with police is not so common. In fact, it's the sort of thing that might make front page news in Scranton even if the event occurred in Houston. Odds were with me.

The riskiest prediction was the third one. At the time racial unrest was widespread. Young blacks in particular were demanding that prejudices come to an end. In fact, I was mistaken about the age—the man involved was not a teenager—but no one noticed.

Finally, almost anyone could have made the prediction about the House vote. It was public knowledge that it would be passed by approximately two hundred votes, and the voting was scheduled in time for headlines on the ninth.

Should you wish to predict headlines yourself, be warned that you will have to do a good deal of homework, and even then a breaking news story of major import might push your predictions to the back pages. First, study for at least two weeks the newspaper for which you plan to predict the headlines. Every newspaper has its own personality. It features particular types of stories; what would be a page one story in one newspaper might be covered in a single paragraph on page six of another. I try to get the feel of the headline writer's style. Will he be brief, long-winded, or "cute"?

Even more demanding, I must have a good knowledge of what's going on locally, nationally, and internationally. Then, using the techniques described in chapter 2, I allow my imagination to play out the major stories. Which will be culminating in a week? Ultimately, it comes down to only a few possibilities. That's when I climb out on a limb.

Although you might not realize it, you make educated guesses every day of your life. You're late for work, and although you usually take the direct route, you know that traffic increases on the main road as the hour grows later. The scenic way is three miles longer, but you'll probably be able to breeze right along. So you act on that educated guess, risking the longer drive to avoid the traffic.

In fact, success in almost every field, as well as in our personal lives, is often the result of making accurate *educated* guesses. And it's as true of big business as of individuals. Large companies spend millions of dollars to test the market for a new product before they begin manufacturing it. But after all the research is gathered and analyzed, the final decision is rendered by high-priced executives who make an educated guess. Often it's a wise decision.

But not always. Ford had its Edsel, *Reader's Digest* its *Families,* a magazine that lived through only a handful of issues before drowning in a sea of red ink. Hollywood has made a life-style of creating blockbuster movies that wouldn't draw an audience even if they were shown free. And then there's Wall Street, the mass economic graveyard of an army of investors who guessed wrong.

Later I'll give you some pointers on what I think goes into making accurate educated guesses and why so many people fail in the attempt. You'll be able to apply this both professionally and personally for dynamic and successful decision making. But first, let's have some fun making educated guesses. (I'm going to cheat and throw in a couple of illusions, too.)

PREDICTABLE RESPONSES

No doubt you're familiar with the psychiatric association test. The examiner tosses out a word and the patient responds immediately with the first word that comes to his mind. "Hat" might elicit "head," "top" might suggest "bottom." The test's value is in the fact that most of us will respond predictably, while those with emotional conflicts might make uncommon associations.

This phenomenon of predictable response can be great fun

at a party. The game can be adapted to several formats. Here's one:

Before the party, write each of the following words on separate three-by-five cards: ROSE, CHAIR, RED, POODLE, BOAT, SUN. (Later you might want to conduct experiments to add to this list; it's most effective when you have twenty to twenty-five cards.) Now memorize the following six words: *flower, furniture, color, dog, ocean, heat.* Learn them in that order.

At the party, try to select a volunteer who is female, intelligent, and not highly creative or imaginative. Ask someone to act as secretary, writing down the volunteer's responses. Say:

"I'm going to give you a word, and I want you to respond instantly with the first thing that comes into your mind. Do you understand?"

Give the first word you've memorized, and be sure the response comes immediately. Allow the secretary to write down the volunteer's answer. Then go on to the next word, and so forth. If the guests are close friends and it's appropriate, you might inject some levity by ending with a word like "bra." As the volunteer hesitates and stammers, laugh and say, "No, forget that. Now, secretary, what was the first response?"

As the secretary responds, turn over the first card. Continue through the list, and chances are you'll hit every time. The longer the list, the more impressive the effect will be.

GUESS THE NUMBER

Give a volunteer a large sheet of paper (eight by ten inches) and a felt-tip pen and ask her to write any number between 100 and 999 on the paper. Tell her that she will have to write additional numbers above or below and she must leave room for that. Then explain:

"I want you to reverse that number in your mind. For example, if you wrote one hundred twenty-three, I want you to think three hundred twenty-one. If the reversed number is *larger* than the original, write it above the first number. Otherwise, write it below. We're simply going to subtract one number from the other." (If the number chosen is the same when reversed, another number must be chosen.)

Ask the volunteer to do just that, writing her answer in large numerals across the bottom of the page.

Although you'll be far enough away from the volunteer so that no one will accuse you of peeking, you can produce a remarkable "mind reading" effect if you can observe the movement of the felt-tip pen as it forms either the first or last number of the answer. Here's why:

The solution to the subtraction problem, no matter what numbers the volunteer uses, will always be one of nine choices. They are: 99, 198, 297, 396, 495, 594, 693, 792, and 891. If there are only two numerals in the answer, you know immediately that it's ninety-nine. If you see that the first numeral is a one *or* that the last is an eight, the answer must be 198. And so forth.

If you cannot distinguish any part of the answer being written, you can still achieve a powerful effect by resorting to a little play acting. After appearing to concentrate with great effort for several seconds, say:

"The first two numbers are very clear. Very clear. I'm having difficulty with the last number. For some reason, I'm blocking it out. I'm going to ask you to tell me the last number."

Let's assume the volunteer says, "Five." You know for certain that the number is 495. Don't announce it immediately. Instead, smile or chuckle and say, "You know—isn't that incredible! I had my tonsils extracted when I was five years old, and I always block that number out." Almost as an afterthought, announce that the number on the page is 495.

A third approach really *does* involve an educated guess. You start with the assumption that the answer is neither 198 nor 891, for although those numbers are possible, they're rare. You simply ask questions:

"Does the answer contain a five?" If so, "Does it end with a four?" From there, you provide the number. Or:

"Does it contain a six? Does it contain a seven?" If you

receive negative answers to each question, it's time to step out on the limb and announce the number as ninety-nine.

TURN OVER COINS

Here's an effect that only appears to be an educated guess. It'll keep your friends guessing all night, but for you it's a sure thing if you can keep your mind on some simple details.

Lay three coins on a table—a dime, a nickel, and a quarter, for example—and start turning them over one by one. Call for a volunteer to continue the process while your back is turned. Explain that he can turn the same coin twice, three times or more, or ignore a coin entirely if he wishes. But each time he turns a coin over (and he must turn only one at a time), he must say: "Turn."

After the volunteer is satisfied that he has turned the coins sufficiently, ask him to cover any *one* of them with his hand, leaving the others in full view. Turn around and examine the two exposed coins. Using your qualities of showmanship, examine the hand covering the coin, or "read" the volunteer's mind to finally announce, "The coin under your hand is showing heads [or tails, as the case may be]."

Many will consider it an educated guess, so you will be required to repeat it time and again until the most hardened skeptic is beaten into submission.

Your success depends on a very simple system, yet one that is virtually never guessed. As you give to the volunteer the coin-turning job, note how many heads are showing. If one or three, you're starting with an odd number of heads. Make this mental note: "Heads—odd." If no heads or two, remember "Heads—even."

As soon as the first coin is turned, the number of heads is automatically changed. If there were an odd number—one or three—there are now none or two. And if there were none or two, there is now one or three. So, with the first turn-over, mentally note the change from heads-odd to heads-even or vice versa.

Your friend can go on turning the coins all afternoon. When he finally stops and covers the coin, the mental note will tell you clearly that there's an odd or even number of heads on the table. By examining the two, you will know what the third is.

If any holdouts refuse to be impressed by your profound achievement, toss another coin onto the table, turn your back and let the flipping begin—*after* observing whether there is an odd or even number of heads on the table. It will work as well as with three coins. If you can carry on some banter about the powers of the mind while keeping track of the heads-even, heads-odd business, you have a right to be proud of yourself. Banter is a sign of the professional, a misdirection that says to the audience (and they believe it): "How can I be paying attention to the coins? I'm talking to you, aren't I?"

COUNT THE FINGERS

I'm including this here because it's effective and it's fun— but it only *appears* to be an educated guess. It's really first-class deceit—or illusion, if you prefer.

Ask for two volunteers. We'll assume you select Bill and Sue. Explain to everyone that while your back is turned Bill and Sue will each choose separately a number from one to five and hold up that many fingers. A closed fist represents the number zero. A third volunteer has the responsibility of silently adding the number of fingers displayed by Bill and Sue and announcing the total. Let's assume the number called out is five. After a moment you explain:

"Bill is holding three fingers and Sue is showing two." And you're correct. You'll be accused of having mirrors on the sides of your glasses, of peeking, of watching the shadows and every other conceivable explanation, so challenge someone to blindfold you, even put your head in a paper bag; you'll still continue successfully every time. The audience might accuse the number caller of somehow tipping you off, so allow the most skeptical to call the numbers. You can even replace Bill. Here's the secret:

You and Sue have a system so simple that it can't miss, yet no one is likely to detect it. In the beginning, when you explain the game, ask for a preliminary test while you watch. You and Sue both make a mental note of the number of fingers that Bill extends during this preliminary test. Suppose that Bill extends two fingers.

When the game actually begins, you and Sue both know that she will extend the number of fingers that Bill did during the practice test—two. When the caller announces that the number is five, it's obvious that Bill has extended three fingers.

Even with your head in a bag, you know that Sue will be extending three fingers in the next test—the same number that Bill showed in the previous round. If the group is large enough, you can even replace Sue, selecting another volunteer who is in on the secret and alert enough to remember the number of fingers that Bill showed last.

THE MATCH GAME

Here's a classic illustration of the educated guess in action, although among some players who achieve extraordinary success, I think it might also demonstrate telepathy.

Ask for a volunteer to be your opponent. Give him three matches and take three yourself. Both of you should be sitting with your hands out of sight under the table. Ask your opponent to put any number of matches he wishes—or none—into his right hand, clench his fist around them, and place the fist on the tabletop. You do the same.

Each player, in turn, then calls a number from zero to six that he believes represents the total number of matches in the fists of *both* players. After each of you has guessed, both open your fists, and whoever guessed correctly wins the game. If both are wrong, it is a tie, and the steps are repeated. Win or lose, the player who made the second guess now goes first.

The first player is at a disadvantage because his guess might well tip his hand so that the second player need only add the matches in his hand to learn the total. For example, if the first player guesses that the total of both hands is zero, he obviously has no matches himself. If he chooses six, he must be holding three himself. If he guesses one, the second player knows that he could not have more than one in his own hand—perhaps he has none. If he says five is the total, he must be holding two or three. If he calls two or four, the guessing becomes more difficult; with two, he could be holding zero, one, or two—and with four, he could have one, two, or three.

When you are the first player, the best number to call is three, for it means that you might have any number of matches in your hand, or none.

The important thing is not to lose the round in which you are the first player. A tie is good enough, and you can practically force the tie by having no matches in your hand and calmly announcing five or six. Your opponent has to assume that you have two or three matches. When he adds that to his matches, no matter what he bids it will be above the actual total. Or, you can use the tactic in reverse, bidding zero while you hold three. Although your opponent will catch on if you do this too often, it will get you into another round in which you get to make the second guess.

The MATCH GAME can be played by as many as seven people, but with some modifications. With three players, the possible totals range from zero to nine; with four players, zero to twelve; with five players, zero to fifteen; with six, zero to eighteen; with seven players, zero to twenty-one. Any player who calls the correct total drops from the game and lets the others fight it out. The game isn't won, it's *lost* by the last player in the game.

LIFE AS AN EDUCATED GUESS

Not long ago I was flying from Los Angeles and the Johnny Carson show to Reno, Nevada, for a week of shows at Harrah's at Lake Tahoe. The first leg of the trip was a short flight from Los Angeles to San Francisco, which should have taken about forty-five minutes. After an hour and a half everyone knew something was wrong, and after two hours I could sense the growing panic. I asked the stewardess what was wrong.

"They can't seem to lower the landing gear," she told me. "We're trying to use up as much fuel as we can in case we have to crash-land." I could sense that she was bravely trying to hide her concern.

"It will be all right," I said without being at all sure myself.

A few minutes later I noticed a settling down among the passengers, an atmosphere that seemed almost serene.

We started in for the landing, dropping altitude. Suddenly we all heard the grinding sound as the landing gear fell into place. It was a perfectly normal landing.

As we were disembarking, I asked the stewardess why the passengers had suddenly grown so calm. She smiled.

"Oh, I just went through the plane telling a few people here and there that Kreskin the mentalist was in the first-class cabin and explaining that you wouldn't have gotten on the plane in the first place if it were going to crash."

She's right, I wouldn't have. And it didn't. But although I've flown more than a million miles in my years as an enter-tainer, I have never had any clairvoyant experiences regarding planes. I take whatever plane is available when I need to go, from jumbo jet to Piper cub. And although the small planes sometimes terrify me, the large ones are another example of the educated guess: large passenger airliners are the safest form of transportation by far, many times less dangerous than the family car. I'll take my chances with planes any day.

There are virtually no actions we can take or decisions we can make in this uncertain life that aren't based on guesswork, from crossing the street to getting married, from raising chil-dren to making investments. *Hoping* for the right result is as risky as spinning the wheel or throwing the dice. Making an educated guess, on the other hand, is far more likely to be successful.

When I talked about predicting newspaper headlines, I actu-ally gave you a four-point program for making accurate pre-dictions in virtually all areas of life. I won't waste time enumerating potential applications of this program, for they're all but infinite. Remember, however, that this is not a method for *influencing* a particular outcome but rather of *understanding* what will occur. It's true that once you have such an understanding, you have greater opportunity to interfere with the natural progress of things and change the outcome. For example, if following the program leads you to predict you'll be fired, you might undertake responsibilities that make you less easily dispensable to the company. The greatest reason for failure in "seeing" the future is our *refusal to face what we don't want to happen.*

For example, with heart-rending frequency we hear of those who deny the serious illness they suffer until it's beyond treatment. We hear of those who build their houses on hills of mud, the slopes of active volcanos, flood plains—and we read regularly of the loss of life and property.

The story is always the same: disregarding the facts of history, common sense, or personal experience, we persuade ourselves, "It really isn't happening the way it seems, it really won't happen that way."

The successful practitioner of the educated guess goes to the facts ruthlessly, completely divorcing what is happening from what he wishes were happening. Only then does he have an opportunity to influence the outcome or at least avoid being damaged by it.

Step One—Know the Facts

Probably the main reason the man in the street has more than his share of failures in business is that his knowledge of the issues involved is incomplete. I once knew a man named Ed who was an excellent chef. After many years of working for others and saving his money, he finally decided to open a restaurant. He found an old building in Chester, New Jersey, and made an agreement with the owner to rent it on a month-to-month lease. He modernized the building at his own expense, doing his own carpentry, and bought thousands of dollars' worth of equipment. He opened with a fine menu, and the most reasonable prices anywhere. Yet for several weeks he had only a trickle of customers.

His first mistake was in not thinking objectively about the location. The building itself was perfect, but it was located on a side road. Although Chester is a vacation area, tourists travel to and from it on the main highway and only rarely explore the road where the restaurant was located. Yet Ed could have survived that mistake and even prospered, for the food was so fine and the prices so low that the restaurant's reputation quickly spread by word of mouth among the locals, who in turn told the vacationers.

After a couple of months Ed's restaurant began to earn a good profit. When the owner saw Ed's success, he invoked his right under the month-to-month lease to raise the rent. Actually, he tripled it. Strapped with start-up loans and operational costs, Ed couldn't pay the increase and lost the business. The landlord anticipated that and became the happy owner of a thriving restaurant.

Ed knew only one fact, and he knew it well: how to cook. It was the facts he didn't know that destroyed his business.

If you're a salesman, know your product inside out—and know the competition's product, too, and why it's not as good. If you're a businessman, understand the widget you're manufacturing but look beyond that to the type of consumer who needs that product. Will some other product serve him better, or will a revolution in the market make your product obsolete? If so, can you build the product that will provoke that revolution? On a larger scale, where is the economy going? And when it becomes tight, will the public still find your widget necessary? If not, can you broaden the company's income base by building an *essential* widget?

The same sort of thinking should go into any investment in stocks, too. That's called studying the *fundamentals,* and it should include not only the company you're interested in but competing companies, the entire industry, and the overall direction of the economy.

Step Two—Know the Psychology

While many investors in stocks follow the fundamentals, others follow the *technical* details and are sometimes called the chart-watchers. They study the day-to-day zigzag movement of stock prices and other factors, and when they recognize a pattern, they make a prediction and give a buy or sell recommendation. That may seem rather irrational and risky, but the technical people have had some solid success. At least part of the reason has to do with the *psychology* involved. Enough investors believe in the charts that when they indicate it's time to buy, these investors *do* buy. Sure enough, the market goes up. The same thing happens with a sell recommendation.

You can make a great many accurate guesses simply by zeroing in on the way the people involved think. Anyone who had the slightest understanding of the nature of Margaret Thatcher and the British people realized from the first moment that England would go to war for the Falklands. It was predictable, given knowledge of the Russian tendency toward opportunism, that since the United States reacted hesitantly when Iran took fifty-two Americans hostage, the Soviet Union would move aggressively as it did in the Afghanistan invasion. And if Muammar Kaddafi of Libya had spent ten minutes analyzing the mind of Ronald Reagan, he would not have lost two planes attempting to bluff the Americans out of "his" gulf.

A good salesman knows within a few seconds after meeting a customer whether he will have a sale or not. He'll know how he must adapt his approach to the personality of the potential customer if he is to increase his chances. The journalist does the same, quickly analyzing the personality of his subject and adapting his approach. He says, in effect, "I can guess from what I've studied about this person and what I'm learning about him right now that if I take *this* tack he won't tell me anything worthwhile. But if I take *that* approach, given his nature, I should be more successful."

Corporate executives and show business personalities often

voice the same complaint: it's not what you can do that counts, but who you play golf (or whatever) with. For better or worse, it's often true, and it says simply that those who understand the *psychology* of the people they deal with are the ones who succeed.

If Ed had spent time trying to understand the mind of the man who owned the building, he might still have a thriving business.

Step Three—Know the Outcome

I won't repeat here what I said in chapter 2 about allowing your imagination full range of expression as you move from the facts and personalities you know and understand to the likely outcome of an interaction of those factors. Be on your guard against intellectual involvement—don't "write the script" you'd like to see played out. Allow the natural course of events to occur in your mind without input from you.

Through this process you can even make good educated guesses about major life commitments. Given the facts you already know and the personality you have, imagine yourself in various careers and play them through to success or failure. If you're contemplating marriage, do you know the man or woman well enough to make a guess in the first place? What are the facts regarding intellectual harmony, mutual interests, tastes, and sexual compatibility? How does the marriage play out?

Step Four—Climb Out on the Limb

"If I'd bought IBM (or Polaroid or Xerox) twenty years ago when I felt so strongly about it, I'd be worth twenty million dollars today." I can't count the times I've heard that sad lament, along with similar ones: "I always knew she'd make a good wife, but while I vacillated, he married her." "I just knew I should have bought [or sold] that house [or stock or land]."

Certainly there's danger in rushing into things, but there's also danger in coming to a full stop on the highway of life. If you're one of those who have difficulty in making a commitment and taking action, I want you to know that I'm not talking here about a leap of faith but an educated guess based on as sound a system as any on earth. By gathering all the facts you can, by analyzing the personalities involved and how they are likely to react under the given circumstances—then, by playing events out in your imagination, you're doing something no computer can do. You're "seeing" into the future with a high probability of accuracy. You can—and should—act on such a conclusion with confidence. You'll hit the bull's-eye far more often than not.

I know that will be true for *you*. That's *my* educated guess.

NINE

First Steps in Telepathy

Some years ago Rita Moreno, Alan King, and I appeared together on the Johnny Carson show. Rita had just won an Emmy award to add to her collection; she has received virtually every prestigious award in show business including a Tony and an Oscar for her marvelous acting talent, but she was not acting that night when she showed her astonishment after witnessing telepathy at work.

Rita, Alan, and Johnny Carson's associate, Ed McMahon, were my volunteers. I asked each of them to put three or four objects on a card table, but before they did so I wrote a statement on a card and, showing it to no one, placed it face down in full view of the studio and TV audience.

Someone placed a watch on the table, someone else a ring. Rita removed an earring. There were some coins. Alan King, always the comedian, removed a shoe and placed it on the table. Finally, Ed McMahon unbuttoned his shirt, loosened his tie and unfastened a necklace he had been wearing. He placed it on the table.

"Rita, will you please pick any item from the table," I said. She paused thoughtfully, reached for Alan King's shoe, then stopped. (I would have stopped, too—who wants to pick up Alan King's shoe?) Again she pondered. She actually touched several items, shoving them aside, then reached into the pile and lifted Ed McMahon's neckpiece.

I picked up the card on which I'd written earlier and held it up to the three volunteers. The TV camera zoomed in on it. Millions of viewers around the country read, "Man's necklace." Rita Moreno screamed. Ed McMahon gaped.

You would probably like to know how that was accomplished. So would I. As I've explained, frequently I myself do not understand how an extraordinary effect like this occurs. But I do think it's unfair to arouse your curiosity without offering at least some possibilities.

First, although Ed McMahon's chain was not visible early on, he must have made me aware of it in some way. Perhaps I actually did get a glimpse of it without consciously realizing the fact. Or I might have seen the shape of it beneath his collar. More likely, Ed McMahon himself communicated the thought of the necklace to me. He would have been very excited about this "perfect" object, since I hadn't seen it and couldn't possibly write it on the card. All I can tell you for certain is that as I picked up the card to write, I *knew* that either Alan King or Ed McMahon would place a necklace on the table. Ed could have spared me a few unsettling moments, however, by putting the necklace on the table immediately!

I can't explain how, by concentrating on the necklace, I led Rita to pick it up. It might be that I had some assistance from Ed, who was certainly convinced I could not have written "man's necklace" on the card, or Rita herself might have come to that conclusion. I believe that Rita, like thousands of others over the years, was influenced by telepathy.

By far the greatest number of so-called telepathic feats performed on the stage and TV are simply illusions—a wonderful form of entertainment and harmful to no one as long as they're not carried beyond the theater and used to bilk people out of their money. Here's a simple illusion of telepathy that you can practice yourself.

Select a young lady from among the partygoers and ask her to stand near a table. Withdraw from an envelope that remains lying on the table three ordinary three-by-five cards. On each card is written a different man's name—common ones such as Jim, Bob, and Dick. Say:

"Without touching any of the cards, choose the name that has played the most significant part in your life. Someone with one of those names has been important to you in some way. Don't touch the card or speak the name yet. Just concentrate on it. Stare at my forehead and concentrate on the name."

After several seconds, ask the volunteer to speak the name aloud. If she says, "Jim," lift the envelope slightly from the table and tell her to reach inside. Ask:

"How many cards are still in the envelope?" She will find one. Say:

"Just one card? And what does it say?"

She will read: "The name of the person important in your life is JIM."

If the name she announces is Bob, turn the envelope over and hand it to her and ask her to read the message that has been written on the underside. It will say: "The person important to you is BOB."

And if she chooses Dick? Ask her to turn all three cards over. Two will be blank, and the third will say: "The person important to you is DICK." Of course, only you know that you've covered all bases—to the others, it's an astonishing example of telepathy.

That was not telepathy, but illusion—and I'll describe some more simple effective telepathic illusions later. But the emphasis in this chapter will be on *actual* telepathic effects, and how you can produce them yourself. Hopefully, you'll be able to demonstrate some rudimentary examples of thought transfer and, if you have the necessary sensitivity, I'll show you how to further develop this extraordinary sense.

My own interest in telepathy began when I was eight years old. In fourth grade we played the game "Hot 'n' Cold" in which one pupil leaves the room while the others hide an eraser or beanbag. When the pupil returns, he begins searching for the hidden object while the others shout, "Hotter! Colder!"

It occurred to me that I'd have a wonderful opportunity to show off before the entire class if I could find the object without any verbal coaching, simply by having everyone concentrate on its location while I somehow read their minds. First, I knew I'd have to practice.

For several weeks my mother and father humored me, but when there was absolutely no sign of success, they grew bored. Then I persuaded my younger brother Joe to try—actually, I'm afraid I bullied him into it—and for about four months we worked at it. By then I was having great success finding almost anything Joe would hide without his giving me any verbal clue. Since that time I've come to suspect that he was directing me by facial expressions—smiles and frowns—since the quicker the tests were completed, the sooner I'd permit him to go out and play. Still there were times when I refused to look in his direction, and I believe I first began to develop the telepathic sense at that time.

I began performing as a magician evenings and weekends the following year, and when I was eleven years old, I included suggestion in my act. But it wasn't until I was about fifteen that I returned—this time with a passion—to my experiments in telepathy. My subjects were usually fellow students, and for the most part they were unaware that I was trying to communicate my thoughts to them or to perceive the foremost thoughts in their minds. Quite often I failed. I can think of at least two reasons. The obvious is that I had a long way to go in perfecting telepathic communication. The second—and you should keep this in mind as you yourself experience failure—is that some people are simply incapable of responding telepathically. Neither you nor I are able to pick up their thoughts, and neither of us will be able to communicate our thoughts to them. As some people are born without sight or hearing, others have no telepathic sense. Or it might be that the telepathic sense is so completely suppressed that it is for all intents nonexistent. Usually, those lacking in telepathic capacity, while not necessarily more intelligent than others, tend to intellectualize all aspects of their lives, including their emotions. You can't *will* your telepathic sense to function; it is an act of the unconscious mind, and the conscious intellect can suppress the unconscious. At least that's my theory, and I'll get back to it later.

By my last year in high school my fellow students were beginning to think me a bit strange. When a close friend called, I would often answer the phone with, "Hello, Nancy," or "Hi, Ralph," which was particularly unsettling to Nancy or Ralph. I'd do it without giving it a thought. I'd meet a friend in the hall and say, "Don't worry about that D minus on the test—you'll do better on the next one." He'd be astonished that I'd known precisely what was on his mind, and when I gave it some thought, I'd be, too.

At that pubescent age young people have a lot of thoughts they prefer to keep to themselves, and I discovered that some of my friends were not at all amused by my ability. They needn't have worried. From some people, as I've said, I can gather no thoughts at all. And telepathic communication can occur only when a particular thought is dominant and the sender is somehow open. I've used telepathy in literally thousands of performances since those high school years, and the most trying aspect is always in selecting subjects who will not embarrass me by blocking the thought transference but who are open and sensitive.

For the following effect it doesn't matter if your subjects are open or not. It's pure illusion. But when we reach actual telepathy tests, choose cooperative, helpful, believing people as subjects.

THE TELEPATHIC MESSAGE
(An Illusion)

The great Dunninger called this "one of the most mystifying spirit effects known." It's a trick, pure and simple, yet few people will ever fathom it.

Begin by passing out slips of paper to six or seven guests. Ask them to write a question requiring advice on a future decision they or someone they know must make. The mediums who use this trick at seances urge that the questions be directed to deceased loved ones whose names be written above the question, but I consider this an unconscionable sham.

Ask the writers to fold the papers so that the writing can't be seen, and collect each note in a hat or bag. Request silence as you withdraw the first question and clutch the paper, still folded, tightly in your hand. Concentrate. Then say:

"Someone is contemplating the purchase of automobile stocks but doubts that this is a wise time for such an investment. Who has asked that question?"

While the writer rises to identify himself, unfold the paper and read it. Then discard it in your pocket. Offer in response some somber-sounding but meaningless platitude such as, "For everything there is a season, but fools rush in where angels fear to tread."

Proceed to the next slip and continue until you have "telepathically" read the questions on all the writers' minds and offered comments.

This is how it's done:

One of the question writers is a confederate. He writes anything—or nothing—on his piece of paper, then folds it in such a way that you will easily recognize it. One method is to tear off a corner of the paper after it's folded so that, even without looking, you can feel the difference. *You must not select this sheet until last.*

After selecting the first sheet and clenching it in your hand, invent any question you like. No matter what the question, your confederate will stand and identify it as his own. To "confirm" the question you've supposedly just read telepathically, open the sheet in your hand and *memorize* the gist of *that* question. When you stuff it in your pocket, the audience believes you're discarding your confederate's question.

After pondering the second sheet of paper, held tightly in your fist, announce the question written on the *first* sheet. Again, as the writer identifies himself, read the next question and discard it.

And so it continues until you withdraw the final paper, the confederate's. Although there might be no question at all on it, you will "telepathically" read the question you've memorized from the previous sheet, thus completing the performance.

The most difficult part of the whole effect is preparing answers that sound profound without saying anything. (Perhaps your local politician will share his expertise in this area with you.)

That was illusion, but now we're going to attempt a few *real* telepathic tests. First I want to give you advice on how to prepare yourself for telepathic communication.

I'm not going to give you my theories here on what I believe might constitute the telepathic phenomenon—I'll reserve that for chapter 11. What you must understand is that it *operates* at a level comparable to instinct. Insofar as civilization has separated us from sensitivity to our instincts, we have also lost our sensitivity to communication without words. Henry deVere Stacpoole, in his book *The Garden of God,* goes so far as to propose that as man relies less and less on speech he becomes increasingly capable of communicating by thoughts with those for whom he cares deeply.

The first step is to free your mind of its compulsion to analyze, judge, conclude—to *intellectualize.* Whenever I fail to do that, I'm in trouble. In Indianapolis, accompanied by United Press International reporters and a local television crew, along with the governor and two high-ranking city officials, I attempted to find a tiny paper decal hidden somewhere in a twenty-five-story building. Only the governor and the officials knew its location, and they served as my silent guides. I told them to think of nothing but the hiding place, and they cooperated fully.

Yet, for fifty-five minutes I faced frustration. My forehead grew damp with sweat as the elevator stopped at floor after floor and the messages I thought I was receiving continued to be garbled, "It's here/it's not on this floor." Intellectually, I knew it *had* to be on some floor. It was not until we reached the twenty-fifth floor and returned to the lobby that I realized that I had reasoned myself into a dilemma. I had been forcing my own question, "What floor is it on?" instead of listening to the answer—"It's not on any floor." I raced back into the elevator, searched it, and found the decal behind the inspection sign.

For the beginner especially, controlling the compulsion to intellectualize is both the most difficult and most essential aspect of telepathic communication. Not only will reasoning force incorrect conclusions, as it did in my search for the paper decal, but it also closes a great many doors that must be left open if you are to receive input. The intellect follows a rigid set of rules, or perhaps many sets, but in the end it boils down to a series of assumptions that *this* means *that*.

When the unconscious is permitted to exert an influence, the input it receives is infinitely more complex and subtle. I am not personally convinced, as some have claimed, that every particle of experience throughout our entire lives is stored somewhere in our unconscious, but I do believe that the information and experience in our unconscious exceeds that of our conscious intellect as the bodies of the universe exceed that of our solar system. And insofar as we allow the unconscious to speak, unblocked by the intellect, we develop and use the telepathic sense.

THE MOVING HAND

Here is an excellent test if you are just beginning telepathic efforts. It requires only one other person, ideally someone with whom you have real harmony of spirit. You will need six cards and a table. Lay the six cards—any six selected at random from the deck—faceup in a row on the table, about two inches apart. Ask your assistant to select mentally just one of the cards, and when he has done so he should announce that he is ready.

Now try to think of nothing at all. Try to envision the pale blue space I described in chapter 2. Hold your hand at least three inches above the outer edge of the first card in the row and move it slowly above each card until you have reached the outer edge of the last card in the row. Pause momentarily before returning in the same fashion to the starting point.

As you continue this process, your hand will have a tendency to dip at some portion of the row. Don't *analyze* this, or your intellect will either exaggerate it or create some rational explanation for it, either of which will interfere with the telepathic communication. Simply slow the motion of your hand until you recognize the single card to which your hand is being drawn. The instant you are certain of the card, pick it up and ask your assistant if that is the one he has chosen.

Statistically, you have one chance in six of choosing the right one, if it were simply a matter of guessing. If you are tapping any telepathic potential, you will find your batting average much better than this, and much too high to be explained as coincidence.

Don't expect the bull's-eye every time. I've been performing this test for many years, and I admit that even today I can't boast infallibility. But if your first choice is wrong, ask your friend to concentrate very hard on the card he's chosen, actually envisioning it. Suggest that he close his eyes if it helps him to concentrate. This time move your hand even more slowly. If there is another person present, ask him to watch your hand while you close your eyes and try to make your mind blank. Ask him to tell you if your hand repeatedly dips, even slightly, over a particular card. If you succeed in your effort, remember that you are still well ahead of the law of averages; you had one chance in five of choosing the right card.

If you fail beyond that, it is for one of two reasons: The obvious is that you're not in touch with the unconscious telepathic sense. An equally strong likelihood, however, is that the tension of the moment—trying to prove yourself to your assistant and any witnesses—is forcing a decision on you before you have received the input necessary to make the proper choice. Under such stress you actually give yourself an autosuggestion that one of the cards is the right one, and acting on it, you make an incorrect choice.

A good opportunity for practicing how to clear your mind of such influence is during a ride on a subway or in any noisy, confused environment. In such a situation rehearse the total relaxation method I give in chapter 2 and see if you can't make the real world momentarily vanish.

AROUND THE CIRCLE

Gather four or five friends around a table and have them each place a couple of objects on it so that there are six to twelve items spread out in a large circle. Be sure they are not too close together, especially if two items are similar—two pens, matchbooks, or whatever. Now say:

"I'm going to leave the room, and while I'm gone, I want you all to agree to choose only one item on the table, the object that you will all concentrate on. Call me when you've selected it."

When you return to the table, remind your friends that each of them must concentrate complete attention on the item that has been chosen. After a pause begin moving your hand around the circle at least three inches above the items.

As you continue, anticipate one of two reactions: You will either sense that your hand is being repelled by some items, like a reverse magnetic field, or you will feel a subtle coolness in some areas of the circle and a relative warmth in others. Unlike the MOVING HAND effect, you will probably not be drawn to the chosen item, but held back from selecting the ones not chosen.

You must therefore use the process of elimination, rejecting that part of the circle that repels you or seems cool. As fewer items remain, you can eliminate them one by one. At this point it becomes difficult to distinguish among the items, so remove the ones already eliminated and spread the remaining ones in a new large circle. Now, without forcing a response, continue the process of elimination until you are drawn to a specific item or feel a slight warmth radiating from it.

Don't be discouraged if you pick the right item only occasionally. If it were a simple spin of the wheel, you would make that right selection only one out of twelve times, on average. In fact, you will probably do much better. More important, if you regularly eliminate 50 percent or more of the items not chosen, even though you might not zero in on the right one, you've certainly demonstrated telepathic ability.

TELEPATHY IN MOTION

The ideal volunteer for this effect is one with a good sense of humor and a tendency to go along with the fun. With that sort of person you're likely to have both a successful effect and plenty of laughs.

Ask the volunteer to stand in the center of a circle formed by the other party guests and close his or her eyes. Explain that the guests are now going to agree on a "target" person, and when that is done silently, by pointing, say:

"Now we're all going to concentrate on 'the target.' In a few moments you [the volunteer in the center of the circle] will begin leaning or swaying, and if we concentrate hard enough, the movement will be primarily in the direction of the 'target.' "

It may take several minutes, but eventually the subject will do just as you predicted. If the subject is not telepathically sensitive, you might have to use suggestion to begin the swaying motion, but more times than not, once begun, it will be in the direction of the "target."

Sometimes the subject actually loses his balance and falls in that direction. Anticipate such remarks as:

"That's nothing—he's been swaying since his fifth martini."

"He's been leaning in her direction all night."

"No, *she's* supposed to lean toward *you.*"

There is much more to be said about telepathy. In fact, I'll return to it at great length in chapter 12. First, in preparation, we must learn more about how the unconscious functions.

TEN

Tapping the Unconscious

Immense hidden powers seem to lurk in the unconscious depths of even the most common men—indeed, of all people without exception.

—FRITZ KIMBEL, Creation Continues

Some months ago I was in the elevator of a hotel in Milwaukee, Wisconsin. Close to me in the crush of passengers going to the upper floors were a middle-aged man and woman who seemed quite agitated. I overheard the woman say, "What do you mean you don't remember what floor we're on? Where's the key?"

The man answered, "I got it here in my pocket someplace." As the elevator continued upward, he searched frantically through pockets in his trousers, jacket, coat, vest. I don't believe I ever saw so many pockets on one person.

The elevator stopped on the seventh floor. The door opened and some passengers exited. As it was about to close again, I pushed the "open" button on the control panel.

"This is your floor," I told the couple.

The man and woman thanked me and stepped off the elevator. Just as the door closed, I saw them look at each other with a sudden flush of astonishment.

Although the story would be perhaps funnier if I could tell you that they were not staying on the seventh floor at all but the fourteenth, the fact is that when I met them in the lobby later in the day they practically accosted me to demand how I'd known their room was on the seventh floor when even they couldn't remember it. I couldn't explain it then and I can't now, but I'll tell you my theory—and it'll be disappointing to anyone who expects me to attribute it to the supernatural. I believe that at some point earlier in the day I was exposed to the information. Perhaps I passed the registration desk as they were checking in and overheard the clerk tell the bellboy, "Room 700." Or I might have been on the elevator with them and seen them get off at the seventh floor. However I gathered those facts, they made no conscious impression. Yet they were held in my unconscious, and although I couldn't have willfully recalled that information for all the money in the world, it flowed out when it was needed.

My own unconscious serves me in a very capricious way, incidentally. It often puzzles my friends and subjects me to ridicule. You see—and this is a confession—I am quite absent-minded and forgetful. At a party, if I take my glasses off and put them on a table, I might spend the remainder of the evening quietly trying to locate them. I'm quite nearsighted, and if they are four or five feet from me I would not be able to identify them. I'm sure that my unsconscious "knows" where the glasses are, but whether I'm playing a game with myself or simply giving myself another lesson in humility, I usually have to ask someone to help me find those glasses.

David Brenner has a favorite story about a mentalist with whom he performed long before he was well-known as a TV and nightclub performer. Although he refuses to admit that the mentalist was Kreskin, I don't mind confessing to it now after all these years, since it so well illustrates my point.

We'd just finished performing at a northeastern university, and I had ended the program as I usually do by locating my check, hidden in some obscure place in the auditorium. After the show David and I had been invited to a private party, and we decided to drive there together in my car. We arrived at least an hour late—it took us that long, wandering through the streets and alleys around the campus, to locate my car. I'd simply forgotten where I'd parked.

The unconscious is *a reservoir of thought of which we are not consciously aware.* Yet it is like the undercurrents of an ocean, or like the jet stream, profoundly influencing all that occurs on the surface. That which shapes our motives and behavior, and contains the real meaning of what we do and who we are, is born in our unconscious.

The knowledge and understanding here is not easily accessible to our conscious selves, and when we do have a sudden glimpse of it, the experience is so remarkable that we sometimes give it a mystical or supernatural interpretation. One fascinating example is *déjà vu,* the conviction of having previously experienced something that you know you must actually be experiencing for the first time. (The term comes from the French and means "already seen.")

Déjà vu is very common. Most of us have felt that we must have been in a particular room before, since everything is so familiar. Yet, logically, it would have been impossible. We've been introduced to people and said impulsively, "Haven't I met you somewhere before?" In fact, we haven't. Some people have participated in entire conversations knowing precisely what they would say and how others would respond and what the final outcome would be. So profound and vivid are some of these experiences that they've given rise to the theory that we've been here, in these same rooms and talking with these same people in a previous life—reincarnation. A few, led on by the suggestion of a "psychic researcher," have recalled minute details of a previous existence.

I have no more corner on the truth regarding reincarnation than you or anyone else. I don't know whether or not such a phenomenon really exists. I *do* know that the evidence for it can be explained as a synthesizing, or joining together, of memories and information stored in the unconscious and rising to our awareness through some triggering factor.

I believe that instances of regression into a previous life are actually the same phenomenon on a more complex scale. The autosuggestion is prodded and reinforced by that of the "researcher," whether through active leading or passive encouragement. The rest is a fantastic process of which not many of us are capable, a drawing together of bits and pieces long buried in that vast reservoir of the unconscious, details we never realized we had absorbed—much like my experience with that couple who had forgotten the floor on which they were staying. That information is culled and collated, and emerges to the consciousness not merely as fact but as experience.

Certainly some claims to previous life regression have been pure fraud, but I believe that in most cases both the subject and the "researcher" have been sincere. I believe they have been sincerely mistaken in their claim to have regressed into a previous life. They merely tapped the unfathomable depths of the unconscious.

THE KRESKIN PENDULUM

In the late 1960s I designed and popularized a device that was sold as a Milton Bradley game called "Kreskin's ESP," and after some years of further development it was reintroduced as the Kreskin Krystal. Basically, these were sophisticated versions of a simple pendulum, a device that legitimately reflects responses of the nervous system—motor responses—to unconscious thought. Many thousands of people have used the Kreskin pendulum to tap their own unconscious beliefs, knowledge, and emotions. In fact, in hospitals all over the world expectant mothers have held a primitive version of the pendulum—a needle dangling by a thread—to determine whether the fetus was male or female. I have no doubt that the production of the hormone testosterone by male fetuses only can be recognized by the mother's unconscious and possibly be expressed through the pendulum.

The Kreskin pendulum consists of a crystal ball one inch in diameter suspended from a fine, flexible chain eight inches long and is ideal for the tests I'll present in this chapter. Or you can make your own simple pendulum by tying an eight-inch length of string around a key or ring. If you hold the unattached end of the chain lightly between your thumb and forefinger with the pendulum or bob dangling freely, your forearm extended and unsupported, a motion will soon occur. Perhaps the pendulum will swing back and forth or to left and right, or it might make a circular motion, either clockwise or the opposite. For a few people the pendulum will stay stock still.

Although it's not our purpose to make the pendulum react to suggestion in this chapter, it can be made to do so. Here's a simple experiment. Lay an ordinary ruler on a table, and near it place an ordinary tumbler or drinking glass. The two should be separated by at least six inches. Ask someone to hold the pendulum directly over the center of the ruler, above the six-inch mark. Instruct the person to gaze steadily downward at the ruler, examining it with complete concentration. Soon, the pendulum will begin to sway left and right, an inch or two at first, then farther and farther to each side until it is traversing most of the ruler's length.

Stop the swinging pendulum and ask the friend to hold it over the center of the glass and concentrate fully on the tumbler's rim. After a few seconds the pendulum will begin to move—not right and left as it did along the ruler but this time in a circular motion. Eventually, its orbit will extend far beyond the size of the tumbler, and the individual holding the pendulum will have no explanation for it.

At a party someone will certainly declare it a fake and insist the volunteer deliberately cooperated. But when the skeptic himself tries it, the chances are good that he'll have the same result. The shape of the ruler and the tumbler provide the suggestion, and without consciously intending to, the volunteer through motor reflexes creates the movement.

But as I said in an earlier chapter, some people do not respond as readily to suggestion as most do. One evening when I was performing at a dinner party, my volunteer was just such a fellow. The skeptic happened to be overweight and had earlier announced that he was on a diet and would eat very little —and not even look at the chocolate eclairs for dessert. For three minutes he held the pendulum over the center line of the ruler, coolly smug. Finally, he declared that it was all a hoax, for the pendulum hadn't moved in the least. I asked him if he wanted to make a wager that the pendulum would indeed move, and he agreed.

I laid a five-dollar bill on the table and asked the hostess to get one of the eclairs from the refrigerator. "If the pendulum doesn't move in sixty seconds, you get my money," I told him. "If it does—" and I laid the eclair on the table and moved his hand so that the pendulum hovered over the center of it— "you'll have to abandon your diet for this evening and eat that eclair."

I knew the five dollars didn't mean anything to him. He was wealthy, and I'd seen him leave that much as a tip for two cups of coffee. The eclair, on the other hand, meant a great deal. He loved them. He *wanted* to eat it. He *wanted* the pendulum to swing, and although I'm sure he didn't do it deliberately, swing it did as he allowed suggestion to take control.

Suggestion might well play a crucial role in bringing unconscious information to the conscious level. In déjà vu, for example, one detail, which I referred to earlier as a triggering factor —perhaps a piece of furniture in a room—*suggests* the possibility of having been in that place before, and as that suggestion is accepted, supporting material is gathered from the unconscious. Although the wallpaper, clock, carpet, painting all might have been seen at different times and places, we merge them together because we have accepted the suggestion of déjà vu in the first place.

That's not to say that the vast powers of the unconscious are merely suggestion or autosuggestion. If we're to tap those powers in a creative and positive way, we must learn to facilitate the flow of thoughts from one level to another by accepting the suggestion that it can happen. *This is the fundamental truth of tapping the power of the unconscious.* It is the key to the promise of Jesus that the tiniest amount of true faith can move mountains. It is not mystical; it is not even essentially religious. It is a simple, pragmatic observation that if you do not open the door, there can be no passage of information.

And so, as you delve into your own unconscious and that of your friends in the pendulum tests that follow, don't be surprised if, rarely, you get no response at all for a few minutes. The pendulum can't be *willed* to work or consciously urged into action—the results will be synthetic and unreliable. It simply must be allowed to function and not resisted.

THE ANSWER SHEET

If you already have the Kreskin Krystal, you needn't prepare the answer sheet. Otherwise, draw a verticle line about two inches long in the center of an 8½-by-11 sheet of paper. In the center of that line draw another horizontally to form a cross. At the top of the vertical line write the word *yes* and at the right end of the horizontal one write *no.* Now hold the chain lightly between your thumb and index finger, your arm away from your body and unsupported. If your arm becomes weary in this position, you can try resting your elbow on the table and bending your wrist until the bob hangs freely one or two inches above the intersection of the two lines. Make no conscious effort to cause the bob to move—or to resist the move. Eventually the bob will begin to move erratically.

INITIAL RESPONSES

Whether you're using the pendulum yourself or demonstrating it at a party, it's wise for you, or the volunteer you call on, to do some warm-up exercises first. Begin by positioning the pendulum and concentrating on the vertical, or *yes,* line. Allow your eyes to move from one end of the line to the other and back repeatedly. In a few seconds, the pendulum will move along that line, indicating *yes.*

Stop the bob with your free hand and position it again. Now concentrate on the *no* line. With no conscious effort on your part, the bob will soon move to indicate *no.*

Rarely, because of individual idiosyncrasies, the bob will move in the horizontal direction to indicate *yes* and the vertical for *no.* In such cases, you must turn the paper to coincide with the individual response, which will be consistent thereafter.

Now concentrate on a clockwise circle, the indication for, "I don't know." The final response to practice is the counterclockwise circle—"I do not wish to answer."

Finally, ask yourself or your volunteer some simple questions with obvious answers. Even if you're alone, ask the questions aloud. Some examples: "Is this the month of March?" "Am I, or are you, married?" "Are there twenty-two inches in one foot?"

The pendulum is a serious tool for prodding your own unconscious and helping it to serve you better in everyday life, but it's also the key to great party fun—even among the always-present skeptics. Here are some of my favorite pendulum games.

THE LIE DETECTOR

Ask the volunteer to write a number—from one to ten—on a piece of paper, and showing it to no one, to slip it into his pocket. Say:

"I'm going to ask you to answer *no* to every question I ask hereafter. Hold the pendulum in position and begin now to concentrate on your answer. Concentrate on *no.*"

The pendulum will soon begin swinging horizontally, along the *no* line. When the motion is obvious, ask:

"Did you write the number *one* on the sheet of paper in

your pocket?" If your subject did not write the number one, the swing of the pendulum will agree with his words when he replies, "No." Otherwise, the pendulum will slowly change the direction of its swing until, while the volunteer insists "No," his unconscious motor reactions will force the pendulum to confess the truth.

Be sure to give the pendulum time to respond before going on to inquire whether the number on the paper is two.

Sometimes the volunteer will impose conscious control over the pendulum. In that case the break from the horizontal plane will be only momentary, but it will be obvious nonetheless. Either way, after you've gone through all ten numbers, you'll be prepared to announce the number in the volunteer's pocket.

You might try some variations on this theme, having the volunteer write a color rather than a number on a slip of paper, or the name of someone in the room, or even an object.

A much more sophisticated and startling variation is really an example of telepathy, or reading another's thoughts as they're made known to you through the subtle movement of the pendulum. There's no trick at all involved—you'll actually be reading the unconscious thoughts of another individual. I've seen people speechless with wonder as a result—and none more so than the volunteer.

Select someone who has had good success with the pendulum previously. Dim the lights somewhat and ask for silence. Tell the volunteer:

"I'm going to name the numbers one through six very slowly. I do *not* want you to think of a particular number among them at this point. You are *not* to think of a number right now, as I mention them. Instead I want you to think of the word *no* after each number. Only later will I ask you to select one. Do you understand?"

Ask the volunteer to position the pendulum. When the bob begins moving vertically, announce the first number. Since you must allow time to elapse while you study the bob, you might say, "The first number is one. Number one. Everyone concentrate on number one." Continue to the next number, and so forth through number six.

What your volunteer and the witnesses don't realize is that, on the unconscious level, your subject already began selecting a number when you told him you would expect him to do so later. And the bob will give that number away when you name it. With some subjects it will change direction totally. With most there will be no more than an erratic warp as the bob begins to pull out of the *no* line for a few swings, then corrects. It's possible that no one else will even notice, but you will.

When you've finished announcing the numbers, ask the volunteer to write secretly any number he chooses from the ones you've mentioned. Simultaneously, you write the number the bob has indicated. Ask the subject to place the paper on the table with the number up, while you do the same.

THE MEMORY TEST

Chances are, most of your friends can't remember the day of the week their last birthday fell on—and perhaps you can't either. Actually, that information is probably still stored in the unconscious, and the pendulum can bring it to the surface. You'll need another piece of white paper. Place a dot in the center of it and write the days of the week in a semicircular fashion around it, like this:

WEDNESDAY

TUESDAY

THURSDAY

MONDAY

FRIDAY

SUNDAY

●   **SATURDAY**

Ask a volunteer to hold the pendulum over the dot. Say: "On what day of the week was your last birthday?" Eventually, the pendulum will begin to swing toward a particular day. The dramatic conclusion, of course, comes when you ask the person for his birthdate, then produce a calendar to prove that the pendulum was correct.

Some of the questions that the pendulum can answer: "What day were you born?" "What day were you married?"

Of course, the pendulum can be used to answer simple questions that the guests might have about themselves or others:

"Do I really want to change jobs?" "Do I feel safe where I live?" At one memorable party a young man handed the pendulum to a girl he'd been dating for some time and asked her casually, "Do you want to marry me?" The bob practically burned the vertical line on the paper. He gave her the engagement ring that night.

Then there was the fellow who asked the volunteer, "Does your wife know you robbed a bank?"

CALLING ON THE UNCONSCIOUS

The pendulum can help you to get in touch with lost memories and buried feelings—and sometimes that can be most useful. For example, suppose you've misplaced your car keys (or, as in my case, your car). Let's assume you know they're somewhere in your home. Mentally divide your home in half, and after relaxing and practicing the warm-up exercises, hold the pendulum over the yes/no cross. Ask yourself aloud, "Are the keys in the front half of the house?" When you get the answer, continue: "Are they in the bedroom?" "Are they in the study?"

When you get a positive response regarding the room, go there and begin the questioning again: "Are they on or in the desk?" "Are they on the sofa?" "Are they on the floor?"

If the keys fell out of your pocket without your knowledge, the pendulum might or might not be useful—it is possible that your conscious mind ignored the sound or sensation while it made an imprint on your unconscious. If you thoughtlessly *put* the keys somewhere, however, there's a very good chance that the pendulum will help you find them.

Perhaps the most important service the pendulum has rendered personally is to help me understand how I really feel about a particular matter so that I can make a wise decision. Sometimes an opportunity that appears on the surface to be a wise move professionally just doesn't feel right to me. Yet I can't understand why. I have great faith in the wisdom of the unconscious, and when the pendulum assures me that I should not make the move, my decision is made. It might be months or years before I understand the wisdom of the decision, before I become aware of all the information that I was weighing and processing unconsciously. But those decisions have always been wise—I wish I could say as much for the conscious ones.

ELEVEN

ESP

There are more things in heaven and earth, Horatio
Than are dreamt of in your philosophy.

—SHAKESPEARE, Hamlet

Earlier I mentioned Bob Kaytes, maitre d' at a nightclub called The Embers near Indianapolis, Indiana. One evening I was performing there, conducting an experiment with a lady from the audience, and within minutes after working with her I abruptly ended the program about halfway through. I don't believe in cheating my audience—if anything, I go overtime—but this was an emergency. Fortunately, since the show was long in the first place, the audience didn't even notice.

The waitresses, however, did—one of the conditions in my contract is that there can be no activity during the concert. Now the waitresses found themselves going back to work sooner than they had anticipated.

Bob Kaytes also noticed. He rushed into my dressing room a moment after I got there and asked me what had happened.

"Bob," I said, "the last person I was working with in the

audience, that woman—get her back here. And get your wife to come back, too. And call a priest or a minister. The lady plans to commit suicide."

I had sensed it almost the way one feels sick to one's stomach, an actual, physical sensation of queasiness that was immediately and consciously associated in my mind with death.

Today I believe that woman came to the nightclub as a cry for help. Perhaps there was no one with whom she could share her feelings, but *if Kreskin could read them,* maybe. . . .

That was about nineteen years ago, and recently I did a fund-raising program to save an old theater in Rahway, New Jersey. I had just found a medal hidden in a grandfather clock in a huge furniture store, and people were gathering around me. Someone touched me, and I felt an unusual sensation. I turned and saw a woman who looked vaguely familiar.

"Kreskin, I want to thank you," she said. "It's because of you that I'm here." It was the lady who had planned suicide.

My brother Joe and his wife Karla live in Florida, and I usually try to visit them during the Christmas season, loaded with gifts. My brother's wife is a fun-loving person, always ready with a joke or a trick. One Christmas I found a most strangely shaped present with my name on it beneath the Christmas tree. The package was actually in the shape of a large U.

"Kreskin, this is one gift you won't *ever* guess," Karla challenged, laughing.

I laughed too. "You're right," I said, "I don't think I could guess it in a million years, unless it's a clock."

She screamed. I was as surprised as she was. It was a grandfather clock, with great clumps of newspaper to give the package its peculiar shape. No one had spoken of a clock. I'm still not sure why I said what I did.

Just recently I was in Dallas, Texas, where a lovely lady reporter interviewed me as part of a local news program. It gave me the opportunity to promote appearances in the area.

Afterward, the two of us were walking through the lobby, and she said she was very happy with the way the discussion had gone.

In the vestibule of the studio, she turned and said, "Kreskin, I want to ask you one more thing."

"I'm Roman Catholic," I told her.

Her jaw dropped. Her eyes widened. "That's what I was going to ask," she said.

"I know," I told her. But I don't know how I knew, or why I know some things and not others.

The three incidents I described are examples of several phenomena known as extrasensory perception—or ESP. ESP includes the following experiences:

Telepathy. Two of the experiences I related were certainly telepathic—that of the woman who planned suicide and that of the reporter who had a question to ask. The third also might have been telepathic, since I might have received Karla's thoughts. The *traditional*—and notice that I'm stressing the word *traditional*—definition of telepathy is the communication of one mind with another by means other than perception through the normal senses.

Clairvoyance. In the final example I gave, the clock itself might have become known to me. The *traditional* definition of clairvoyance is knowledge of an object, person, or event acquired without the use of the normal senses.

Precognition. This is the gift that fortune-tellers, seers, and prophets claim to exercise—knowledge of the future. Knowledge of future events is called precognitive clairvoyance; that of future thoughts is precognitive telepathy.

Psychokinesis. This is the ability to move objects or affect the course of events through mental rather than physical power.

I have emphasized that the above definition of telepathy and clairvoyance—and, by implication, precognition—are those traditionally held. They are not held by me. Neither is the traditional definition of ESP.

What are *my* definitions? I'll tell you, but understand that, my experience notwithstanding, this is merely one man's theory. And it doesn't satisfy even me fully. Perhaps it will provide food for thought, but I hope you won't swallow it whole.

First let's establish this: a phenomenon that at least *resembles* extrasensory perception certainly exists. Every culture for which we have records at every point in history has included members who have demonstrated or claimed abilities now called ESP.

And they were taken seriously. In Middle Ages Europe and pre-Revolutionary America people who demonstrated psychic powers were considered in league with the devil and burned at the stake.

In the nineteenth century critics became more sophisticated. Psychics were no longer evil—merely insane. Today they're usually dismissed as frauds.

I have deep respect for those who have sincerely and carefully examined ESP and remain skeptical, but nothing arouses my anger more than the arrogance of a cavalier dismissal of *any* subject, including ESP, simply because "it can't be true." Thus were dismissed the teachings of Socrates and Jesus, the observations of Galileo, the genius of Chopin and van Gogh.

There is much in the history of the race for which we of the human family can be ashamed, but perhaps the most tragic and shameful is what has resulted from our haughty self-assurance. The path of years is cluttered with examples. One that has long haunted me is that of the Hungarian obstetrician Ignaz Semmelweis, who died when he was only forty-eight years old. When Semmelweis began delivering babies, the mortality among mothers was almost 20 percent. The deaths usually were caused by bacterial infection, but no one knew anything about bacteria then. Through a chance observation, Semmelweis concluded that indeed there was some invisible substance being carried from ill people to healthy ones and causing sickness and death. Thereafter he insisted that everyone—student or physician—entering his obstetric ward wash his hands thoroughly with an antiseptic solution. He also washed all instruments thoroughly.

The results were astonishing. The mortality rate dropped to a record low. Later he taught thousands of students the technique of antisepsis and performed major surgery successfully in a sanitary environment.

But the medical establishment of all Europe rejected his views and continued to deliver babies and perform operations with hands unwashed, killing thousands. So vitriolic were the criticisms and insults hurled at Semmelweis for suggesting that unseen substances exist, the man's spirit and mind finally shattered and he died insane.

Each of us wears blinders. If this book has illustrated a single truth, it is that. Our vision is limited because, even for the Einsteins among us, our *intellects* are limited. If we were to rely more on our unconscious, that would expand our understanding—but even the unconscious has its limitations. The wise man or woman recognizes consciously and continuously the shortcomings of his or her intellect and is quite loathe to give snap answers to complex questions. There is always room to doubt facts that everyone "knows," and to consider the "impossible."

ESP DEFINED

I am a conservative in an extravagant field. That will be obvious when I state what you've perhaps already suspected: when I use the term ESP, I do *not* refer to extrasensory perception. To my way of thinking, ESP is *Extremely Sensitive Perception*. I explained this in some detail in a recent interview with *Psychic* magazine in response to the question: "Are you psychic?"

If you're asking if I manifest phenomena that fit in the category of being psychic, I would say yes, under certain conditions. But I would prefer to say that what I do is hypersensitive or hypernormal, rather than extrasensitive.

I think a great deal of phenomena in the field of parapsychology is related to the senses in terms we've never been able to compartmentalize. We have blurred it by saying it's ESP.

If a person thinks about it, ESP is an abortive contradiction. It suggests that we have an ability to perceive beyond our senses. How can we have a sense beyond our senses? Maybe we should just expand the five senses to six or seven or even 22.

So in this light, I would say that I do manifest some of what we call ESP. But I don't do it under *any* conditions; I have to control my conditions.

I call this extreme sensitivity *hyperesthesia*. I must explain that, when used as a medical term, hyperesthesia means abnormally extreme, even painful, sensitivity to touch, heat, and cold. I'm defining the word as it was used by the British Society of Psychical Research—extremely sensitive development of the ordinary senses, usually on an unconscious level among relatively rare individuals.

ESP may be nothing more or less than that.

That means that the whole debate over whether or not ESP really exists is a comedy starring both skeptics and proponents of ESP. Each has spent a great deal of time and money in the last fifty years in efforts to prove or disprove the existence of ESP. The question remains unresolved—because it is the wrong question in the first place. The question that needs studying is: "What actually happens to produce an 'extrasensory' phenomenon?"

HYPERESTHESIA AND ESP

Recently, twelve mothers lined up to face twenty-four slightly used T-shirts. Each of the mothers had two children, each of whom had worn one of those shirts to bed the previous three nights.

At a signal the mothers examined the shirts carefully. There were no identifying marks. Yet through some extraordinary means, eight of the twelve mothers identified the shirts belonging to their children.

Then later the children themselves took part, and nineteen of the twenty-four were able to identify their brother's or sister's shirt.

Smell

A classic example of clairvoyance? Yes, but not steeped in the supernatural or extrasensory. The study was undertaken by psychologist Richard H. Porter of Vanderbilt University Medical Center and was designed to show how sensitive our sense of smell really is. Both mothers and children relied on odor to identify the shirts. Previously, the mothers had probably not even been conscious of their children's body odors, but the fact was retained in the unconsciousness of at least two-thirds of them.

The old-time mesmerists often produced a similar effect. After "mesmerizing" a subject, the performer would present him or her with an object belonging to a member of the audience. The volunteer would examine the object, hold it close to his or her face, move out into the audience, and eventually find the person who owned the object. Suggestion was probably very important to the success of this effect, for it allowed the volunteer to set aside the intellect and become aware of information usually held in the unconscious. In this case the information was the odor of the object, so subtle that most of us would not consciously recognize it, either on the subject or the person who owned it. Yet the mesmerist's subject did.

You can produce virtually the same effect yourself at a small party. Have the guests contribute one personal item each at the outset—earrings, pipe, tie clip, and such—and explain that you will later identify the owners of some of the items. (Of course you must not look while the objects are being contributed. Although that would make it much easier for you, the partygoers would not be particularly impressed with your skill.)

When the items have been gathered, inspect them carefully, particularly for odor. Earrings will probably carry a faint perfume scent. Pipes, cigars, and cigarettes will have a distinct odor. Coins might carry a delicate trace of aftershave lotion or cologne, since men usually apply those substances with their hands.

Later, milling with the guests, link the smells you remember with the guests who produced them. The more information you retrieve from your unconscious, the more successful you'll be.

Touch

I have a friend who lives alone on a small, secluded farm in the country, and since his retirement some years ago he has been in a more or less perpetual state of undress. As a result, my friend says he can "hear" and "see" more than he ever imagined possible. I've actually seen him reach back to pet his dog, without looking, although the animal hadn't been there a few seconds earlier.

"I feel the heat of his breath on my leg when it's cool out," he explains. Yet the dog had been three feet away from his leg.

I've seen him turn to look at a bird that had landed ten feet away, behind him. The hair on his body had been stirred by the slight breeze. I've seen him sit and rise again, saying, "Sorry, you were sitting here—the chair's still warm." And he's noticed when people were moving in an adjacent room—a slight breeze fluttered across his body.

Acute awareness of tactile sensation can help *you* to "see" and "hear" more, too—and it isn't necessary to be undressed. In fact, here's a good way to conclude the clairvoyance effect that relied on smell, which I described above.

After you've identified the owners of the most obvious items through olfactory hyperesthesia, ask someone whose contribution you have not identified to step forward. Say:

"When I turn my back, I want you to pick up the item belonging to you, hold it tightly in your fist and press the knuckles of your fist against your forehead. I want you to concentrate on the item, projecting to my mind what it is you're holding."

After the subject has followed your instructions for at least twenty-five seconds, and while your back is still toward her, ask her to put the object back on the table and return to the group. Now turn around and approach the table.

Perhaps you'll notice immediately that one object is not precisely where it had been—visual hyperesthesia. Most intelligent volunteers won't give you that advantage, however. Instead, you'll have to pick up each item and hold it in your fist, concentrating. If all the items have rested on the table for several minutes, they'll be at room temperature—or lower if you've placed the table in front of an air-conditioner. The item that has been held in the palm of the volunteer, however, will be close to 98.6° F, rather than the typical room temperature of 72°. That's a significant and noticeable difference, making it easy for you to identify the item. The process can be continued with each guest until every item has been returned to its owner.

There is no end to the ways that a highly developed sense of touch can be used. In the days before X rays and blood analysis, medical doctors routinely made accurate diagnoses by smelling the patient's breath and urine, examining the color of his tongue and skin—and *touching*. Was the skin dry and leathery? Damp and sagging? Cool or warm? Each answer narrowed the potential diagnosis.

Here's a game you and your friends can enjoy while improving your tactile hyperesthesia. Have the game host fill one small plastic sandwich bag with ice cubes, and stuff three additional bags with wooden blocks the same size as the ice. (Lacking blocks, you can fill watertight bags with very hot and very cold water.)

Spread the bags across a table so that they're several inches apart. Have each player hold his hand at least three feet above the bags and move back and forth until he is ready to identify the bag containing the ice, or cold water. If it becomes too confusing to have all the players moving together, you can also use a timing system. When the player feels he can make the identification, he stops and writes his answer, but doesn't make the announcement aloud. The host also records the length of time each player took. If no player can make an accurate guess at three feet from the bags, the host should lower the distance gradually.

A similar game can be played with bricks. One brick can be put out in the sun for twenty minutes, or in the oven. The object is to identify the heated brick. It's easier than you might think.

Hearing

People don't listen to each other anymore. I'm not sure that they ever did, but today it's become almost a basic fact of life. We keep the television blaring but ignore it. We say to strangers, "How are you?" "Have a nice day," without caring in the least how they are or what their day turns out to be like. And the ultimate noncommunicative talk is at a cocktail party. It's for this reason, and the fact that they're extraordinarily boring, that I rarely attend cocktail parties anymore.

In the past I'd keep myself awake at such events by conducting a little experiment that nobody but myself and one companion was privy to. I would approach the welcoming line of key officials, politicians, celebrities, executives, or what have you, shake hands vigorously, and say something to this effect:

"Did you really enjoy the performance? Well, thank you very much. I raped your wife earlier this evening, and hope I'll be able to meet you again. I'll be back in this city in two months, in fact."

The companion at my side usually turned ashen, for my "confession" was as clear and articulate as anything else I'd said. But the gentleman to whom I was speaking wasn't *listening*. He didn't expect to hear what I'd said, didn't want to hear it, and simply didn't.

Most of us have no trouble hearing—our problem is in concentrating, separating the noise from the message. There's no better place to develop listening concentration than on a crowded bus or subway, where scores of conversations are taking place at once and all are buried beneath the grinding and screeching of machinery. Allow yourself to relax, then concentrate passively on the one conversation you're attempting to distinguish.

Another way to develop auditory hyperesthesia is by turning the radio down lower and lower until you have to make a real effort to hear it. After five or ten minutes, you'll find that you're hearing more and more. Turn it down again. Now you might hear nothing for as long as twenty or twenty-five minutes. Then you'll notice that you're indeed hearing certain words and phrases. As you continue practicing day after day, your hearing will become more acute.

You can use your wristwatch for the same purpose, if it's the kind that makes a ticking sound. Hold it in front of you and listen for the ticking. When you're certain you hear it, move it farther away. Or put the watch down and back away from it. Mark the farthest point at which you can still hear the watch. Make yourself comfortable at that point and simply relax, concentrating. Chances are good that after a few minutes you'll begin picking up the sounds of the ticking again.

If you're the kind who loves to share in juicy gossip (I'm not), improved hearing sensitivity might make cocktail parties fun for you after all. There's no end to the tidbits that pour out of people when they think no one else can hear them.

Sight

I have spent many hours riding in police cruisers through block after block of dangerous and squalid inner cities in an effort to help the police discover leads in difficult cases. And one of the things that has impressed me a great deal is the alertness of the officers who work these areas every day. They recognize instantly tiny details that most of us would ignore— a door ajar, a drawn shade, a nervous twitch in an otherwise emotionless face. Often when an officer interrupts a crime in progress, he himself doesn't know what prompted him to investigate. One officer told me it was just a hunch, another said he had some vague suspicion. I believe it was visual hyperesthesia recognized by the unconscious and rising to the consciousness only as an uneasy suspicion or hunch.

For all their mumbo-jumbo and incantations, those old mesmerists produced some quite effective results. One of the most startling effects involved several blank cards—six, twelve, or more. The cards were all of the same size, made of stiff cardboard and absolutely identical to the average observer. The mesmerist, through flamboyant gestures with his cape and wand, would lead a subject to deep concentration and suggestibility. He would then hold up one of the cards and tell the subject that it was a photograph of someone that the subject loved dearly.

The volunteer would study the card carefully, "seeing" on the blank card the photograph the mesmerist had suggested. The mesmerist would then approach the audience and, out of sight of the subject, mark with an X the back of the white card that supposedly was the photograph.

The mesmerist would then shuffle the cards and spread them across a table. "Will you please pick up and hand to me the photograph of your beloved?" the mesmerist would request of the subject. Invariably, usually without hesitation, the subject would pick a card and hand it to the mesmerist—who in turn would display for the audience the X on the back of the card.

It's easy enough to perform this effect through old-fashioned illusion, but that is not how it was done. While each of the cards seemed to be identical, they were not. There were natural, random differences—wrinkles, rough edges, smudges—that made each subtly unique. When the mesmerist commanded the subject to concentrate fully, those characteristics that set the "photograph" card apart from the others were absorbed into the subject's unconscious. He was never aware that he'd seen them, but he had. They and the imaginary photograph had become one, and it was a simple matter to identify the proper card.

Here's an effect of visual hyperesthesia you can perform for your friends. Have three or four people stand near one side of a table. Place a quarter on the table before them. Explain the following instructions so that everyone understands and follows them precisely:

"When I turn my back, I want you to agree among yourselves that *one* of you will take that quarter in his hand, clench it tightly in his fist, press his knuckles firmly against his forehead and concentrate on these words: 'I have the coin in my left [or right] hand.' The person with the coin will keep his other hand at his side, his fingers open.

"The rest of you will also keep your hands at your sides with your fingers open, while you concentrate on these words: 'My hands are open and empty. I do not have the coin.' When you have done that for *twenty seconds,* I want you all to say: 'Now. Ready.' "

When the group announces that your instructions have been followed and they're ready, direct them without turning around to hold their hands in front of them, fists clenched, at waist level. Explain that you will tell them what hand is holding the coin. Turn around, and proceed to do that immediately.

Actually, it will be quite simple. If four people are playing, only one of the eight hands will appear a lighter color than normal, and it will probably be the only hand that does not have veins bulging. The others, which were all hanging at the sides, will show obvious signs of pooling blood.

To view ESP as hypersensory rather than extrasensory is not to reduce its significance at all. On the contrary, it makes possible, finally, serious in-depth investigation. Just one example: For thousands of years, some people have claimed to be able to predict earthquakes. Others have called them fools, frauds, or maniacs. That was the extent of the debate.

Recently, Dr. Helmut Tributsch, professor of physical chemistry at the Free University of Berlin, wrote *When the*

Snakes Awake, published by the MIT Press. Tributsch's carefully researched argument is that oxen, sheep, dogs, geese, and many other animals—including snakes—sense certain prequake seismic events days or weeks before the quake actually occurs and flee the area. If that's true, certainly hyperesthetic humans could detect the indications, too. It's an area of extreme practical importance, and now that we have some idea what's really happening when a "sensitive" predicts an earthquake, we should seek to develop and benefit by this ability.

I believe that most people can achieve a level of ESP (Extremely Sensitive Perception) far beyond their expectations. As with any skill, it requires real effort. I've spent a lifetime at it, and I learn more every day. It will require *time, attention,* and *motivation*—although if you have practiced all that I've discussed thus far, you're already farther ahead than most people will ever get.

You must be dedicated—and you must be realistic. The wide-eyed believer in magic is probably already tuned out—he plays the lottery, prays for miracles, and has no intention of working for anything that he can daydream about with equal satisfaction. I have more confidence in the open-minded skeptic, who, if he has come this far with me, will be demonstrating ESP himself before long, even beyond the experiments I've presented. The only enemy he must guard against is narrow-mindedness. He must learn to ask, in this and in all areas, not "Can it be so?" but *"How* can it be so?" Otherwise he is like an artist who is color-blind, a musician who is tone-deaf.

In my experience those most likely to demonstrate ESP are neither skeptical nor gullible. They are simply *open.* They have no difficulty with reality, nor with fantasy or imagination. They can face frustration and even tragedy, analyze and solve problems, yet move easily to the realm of the imagination we've explored in chapter 2. Such people *like* themselves and *understand* themselves, and they are not frightened of what might exist in the unconscious. They have a curiosity about their own minds. They tend to be friends with themselves—

and there are fewer people who feel that way than you might guess. Exploring their own unconscious is a pleasure for them, and the time they invest keeps the communication lines open and the information flowing.

In a nutshell, I think that those who would experience ESP must recognize that there is a great deal more in the world—and in the mind—than is apparent. Perhaps they do not believe—but they are open and willing and *prepared* to believe.

TWELVE

Where Are We Going?

And now here is my secret, a very simple secret:
It is only with the heart that one can see rightly:
What is essential is invisible to the eye.
— SAINT-EXUPÉRY, The Little Prince

In recent years, while performing at hundreds of colleges and universities all over America, I've discovered that young people today are frightened. They're afraid of "the bomb," of irrational violence, economic and political chaos around the world, their own futures personally and professionally.

"Kreskin," they ask, "what is the future going to be like?"

My first response, as I've already said, is that I'm not a fortune-teller or psychic. I can't "see" into the future. What I *can* do—and have done—is to make the educated guesses I discussed in chapter 8. They're typically more accurate than the best-known "seer" 's predictions.

With that qualification, here are a few of my expectations for the future.

It's my "guess" that the most significant advances world-wide during the next twenty-five years will be not in computers or genetics or space exploration but in developing and utilizing the power of the human mind. At present, the science of mind is but an embryo. We have been so busy with the physical sciences, with material advancement, that, to use an unintentional pun, we haven't even given the mind a thought. The psychiatric community is at pains to *define* the various emotional illnesses, much less to treat them in an agreed upon, scientific manner that can be verified and duplicated. At best the mental health profession is an art, at worst a fraud—certainly not a science.

I believe we are at the threshold of change in the mental health field. We are finally beginning to take the mind seriously, to recognize that there is a virtually unexplored, virtually unutilized universe of wonder and potential there. And as we begin to learn about and use this potential, our lives will change profoundly.

THE BUSINESS OF LIVING

A few years ago on the "Mike Douglas Show," I asked several top sports figures and one police officer to stand eight feet from a hanging tire tube and throw a ball through it. Each of them did so repeatedly and with no difficulty. Then I said to them:

"If I told you now that you could *not* throw the ball through that tube, that you would fail at so easy a task, do you think that you could do it?" A few smiled and nodded, and the rest laughed and said, "Certainly."

I asked them to think of the most upsetting, distressing, and traumatic experience of their lives. It took a few of them thirty seconds to decide what to think about, but finally they all assured me they had such an incident in mind. I asked each of them to continue to keep the experience in mind as they took turns throwing the ball.

They obeyed—and not *one* was able to get the ball through

the tube. Most of them missed the tire by great distances, and one actually threw the ball over his head and behind him.

The implications of that tiny piece of entertainment are far reaching and of critical importance. Those men miserably failed to fulfill their potential because I forced them to relive severe emotional trauma.

Millions of young people today are failing in the same way to live up to their potential, for the same reasons. Living on the wrong side of the tracks does not create failed lives. Neither does economic deprivation or crowded homes. When those factors lead to severe emotional trauma—*then* they produce young people who cannot succeed in the world.

The Bible speaks of the sin of the fathers visited onto the third and fourth generation, and that's precisely what we see in so many families today: fathers who themselves were abused and abandoned by their fathers passing on the heritage of abuse and abandonment to their children, who in turn brutalize and abandon. Emotional trauma becomes a way of life, short-circuiting the brilliant potential of youth.

I predict that within no more than ten to twelve years the social services will make harmony and tranquillity first priorities in young lives. The concept of the unfit parent will be reexamined in light not of external laws but the child's happiness. Both foster children and problem youngsters will be permitted a new sense of permanence and stability rather than be subjected to the current practice of constant relocation and the emotional trauma that entails.

I believe there will be great upheaval in the educational system, beginning almost immediately. The public is already rebelling against the paradox of increased taxes and declining scholastic achievement. Taxpayers will demand educational objectives that go beyond baby-sitting. They will expect the schools to mold character, instill purpose, ignite spirit—in short, to prepare youngsters to play a positive role in society. Many people have already come to realize that the most highly trained intellect linked to a sick spirit usually amounts to a failed life.

From the first day a child enters a classroom he will begin hearing about his own marvelous potential to succeed. Teachers will learn how to plant positive suggestion, how to infuse young minds with values and goals. And if that sounds like Big Brother to you, let me repeat something I said in an earlier chapter: every one of us accepts subtle suggestions every day of our lives. The question is simply this: should the suggestion be the invidious, propagandistic, destructive distortions of a subculture, too subtle to be identified and exposed, or socially positive influences offered in the classroom. I believe we will not only prefer but demand the latter.

I believe there will be a fascinating change in the gadgetry of our lives. Anyone familiar with biofeedback research knows that a change in brain waves—either conscious or unconscious thought—can cause a buzzer to sound, a light to go on, or by extension virtually any mechanical effect to take place. I believe that within a score of years we will be controlling a great many mechanical processes purely by thought. The technology will be marketed first as simple curiosity-type gifts, but it will rapidly be applied in emergency auto safety devices to provide instant braking.

As Gallup, Harris, Presidential candidate Dewey, and political parties around the world have discovered, polling and surveying, sophisticated as they have become, are still imperfect sciences. The reason is that we don't always tell an interviewer what we really think. Perhaps the interviewer doesn't even ask us the right question. Or perhaps we don't *know* how we feel "deep down."

Sometime in the next century survey takers will ask our permission to tap into a very limited area of our thoughts, those pertaining to the survey subject. Through bioelectronic means the interviewer will gather a printout that will explain not only how we feel about particular issues but how strongly and to what extent we are likely to change our minds.

There is great negative potential to technology that allows access to even unconscious thoughts. Some will seek to apply it to mental patients and convicts to learn whether or not they are rehabilitated and can safely be released into society. Others will vehemently oppose it as utterly destroying privacy. Rigid federal regulations will be established before the technology is licensed.

In professional sports every team will have a "mind coach." His primary responsibility will be to teach players the art of imagery in daily *pre-experiencing sessions* of the forthcoming game. So effective will this prove in actual competition that it will be an integral part of all athletic training.

Business counselors will have a similar function, guiding executives in using imagination and unconscious knowledge to find dynamic, creative solutions and ideas.

MIND AND HEALTH

We will see a genuine revolution in mental health. The sun is even now setting on psychoanalysis as a form of psychotherapy. I don't know any psychologists today who honestly believe in Freudian psychoanalysis. Freud's greatest work was in describing and categorizing neuroses, a contribution that will always be considered classic; his therapeutic theories were not particularly successful even when *he* applied them.

What's more, psychotherapy is a luxury that fewer and fewer can afford. Therapists typically charge $75 to $100 a session, and therapy frequently continues for years. I'm not sure whether the economic hardship this thrusts upon most patients increases the severity of their illness or motivates them to get well more quickly, but I am sure that the fees are unconscionably high for a treatment modality based on no more scientific evidence than palm reading or a seance.

Here's a fact that might surprise you. Studies have shown that no matter what type of therapy is used—psychoanalysis, hypnosis, dream analysis, persuasion therapy, transactional analysis, or what have you—about one third of the patients achieve complete rehabilitation. Another third improve moderately, and the final third show no improvement.

Anecdotal evidence suggests that at least as high a success rate—perhaps higher—can be achieved by a voodoo doctor, a witch, a minister, or the woman down the street to whom everyone can tell their troubles in confidence. It isn't the *mode* of therapy that works, it's the mental dynamics of two people interacting.

I predict that psychotherapy will become much more *directive,* dealing specifically with the emotional complaint, and emotional problems will be dealt with as decisively as bodily ailments now are. The great advances will be made in the use of autosuggestion and visual imagery. The effective psychotherapist will lead his patient to vividly *pre-live* aspects of his life that cause phobic or neurotic reactions and, distanced from the reality of them, learn ways to cope with them. He'll help his patient to accept positive, healthy suggestion for improving mood, self-image, and such.

Dramatic advances will be made in the area of neurochemistry. Already pioneering researchers are treating some forms of mental illness by reestablishing the normal biochemistry of the brain to eliminate bizarre behavior and restore normalcy. Findings in this area within the next decade will far surpass the expectations of even the most optimistic researchers of today.

We've seen the end of the "Me" generation of the sixties; although it made many publishers wealthy, it simply didn't work. Putting the spotlight on ourselves, with all our frailties and defects is no way to find happiness, security, and self-confidence. Instead, in the immediate future the emphasis will be on helping others, and psychotherapy will involve to an increasing extent not only the patient but also his family, friends, and colleagues—all of whom will voluntarily participate in an intensive behavioral/thought-conditioning program.

I anticipate that quite soon the Sleep Temples of ancient Greece and Rome will find their way into our modern culture, providing much-needed facilities while making a number of people very wealthy. They will be dimly lit, private rooms where the weary traveler can retreat for privacy, relaxation, and sleep. The user will select any of several sounds—mystic chanting, music, wind, sea. Or silence. He will choose total darkness, a pastoral scene, or a pendulum on which to focus his attention while he grows progressively more relaxed and finally sleeps.

Sleep Temples will be located at airports, in city centers, even along highways. Only one individual will be permitted per room, and the fee will be very moderate, perhaps five dollars per hour.

In Russia similar facilities have been provided in certain cities for about two decades.

Attitude-based medicine will become a recognized field of medical specialization. Today many authorities around the world feel strongly that a negative mood can significantly extend recovery periods and even make the difference in a critical situation between survival and death. Soon practitioners will determine the patient's attitude through carefully designed profiles before allowing surgeons to operate. Patients who are excessively frightened, depressed, or apathetic will undergo emotional rehabilitation, including positive suggestion and imagery integration before surgery is permitted.

Some so-called physical ailments will be routinely treated through very intensive mind conditioning. There now exists, for example, a psychological profile of cancer victims, including depression, a lack of sense of humor, and a defeatist attitude. Treatment will aim at changing negative emotional factors in order to stimulate the defense mechanisms that prevent or arrest cancer.

Within the next century it will be possible for some people to tune in to their inner selves and inner feelings so profoundly that they will be able to monitor subtle functions of their bodies. They will recognize a sense of inner health and strength, or inner weakness and disease—and actually be able to diagnose physical maladies before symptoms become obvious.

We will learn to use color to influence positively all aspects of our lives. We will use light blue, gray, and pale green rooms for personal relaxation and tranquillity; bright-colored rooms to stimulate imagination, create beauty, and passion; beige and yellow rooms to induce concentration. By use of lighting we will instantly change the color of our living areas to coincide with our moods—or therapeutically, to eliminate depression or boredom and create positive feelings.

It's conceivable that within the next decade pain will be a rare phenomenon, whether the problem is a toothache or a ravaging ulcer. The relief will result not from drugs but from a deeper understanding of what actually occurs in acupuncture, hypnoanesthesia, and the "spell" of the witch doctor. Millions of people will learn the simple art of autosuggesting pain away.

I AND THOU

On a scale unprecedented in human history we will see efforts to manipulate the human mind. Appeals to the unconscious will be used in TV commercials and magazine advertisements, and by Jim Jones–type preachers, politicians, and governments. The weaker democratic nations will be threatened as the Soviet Union wages war through propaganda so subtle and sophisticated as to be unrecognizable yet effective mind control. Corporations will attempt to persuade the public to accept unconscionably high profits and pollution of the environment as essential to prosperity. By using mass-suggestion techniques they will succeed with many.

A free press and citizens alert to the techniques of suggestion will strive to keep the masses informed of the truth through a vivid and dynamic presentation of facts. But the ultimate weapon against deceit of all sorts will be the growing potential of every person to understand his own mind and the minds of others. Thought perception will make lying, scheming, and cheating as obsolete as the horse and carriage.

Openness and integrity will be not only the ideal but ultimately the only possible means of dealing with each other. Recognizing the essential unity, the basic oneness of human consciousness, will lead the Western world to a renewed balance of the material and spiritual realms that has been lacking for more than a century.

For too long it has been the hallmark of intellectualism to see the world as plunging headlong toward destruction. I hold a far brighter expectation, one in which we share in humility and openness a nature created in the image of God.

I believe that such a world exists in our future, and that—searching the uncharted reaches of the mind—we will find it.